DISGUSTING SCIENCE

Glenn Murphy wrote his first book, *Why Is Snot Green?*, while working at the Science Museum, London. Since then he has written around twenty popular-science titles aimed at kids and teens, including the bestselling *How Loud Can You Burp?* and *Space: The Whole Whizz-Bang Story*.

These days he lives in sunny, leafy North Carolina — with his wife Heather, his son Sean, and two *unfeasibly* large felines.

SCIENCE SORTED

DISGUSTING SCIENCE

A REVOLTING LOOK AT WHAT MAKES THINGS GROSS

NOM NOM

GLENN MURPHY

Illustrated by Mike Phillips

MACMILLAN CHILDREN'S BOOKS

For Heather and for all the hardworkin' mums and dads
out there – dealing with snot, poo and disgusting things on a
daily basis and loving their little'uns through it all!

First published 2014 by Macmillan Children's Books
a division of Macmillan Publishers Limited
20 New Wharf Road, London N1 9RR
Basingstoke and Oxford
Associated companies throughout the world
www.panmacmillan.com

ISBN 978-1-4472-5299-3

Text copyright © Glenn Murphy 2014
Illustrations copyright © Mike Phillips 2014
Design and doodles: Dan Newman

The right of Glenn Murphy and Mike Phillips to be identified as the
author and illustrator of this work has been asserted by them
in accordance with the Copyright, Designs and Patents Act 1988.

1 3 5 7 9 8 6 4 2

A CIP catalogue record for this book is available from the British Library.

Printed and bound by CPI Group (UK) Ltd, Croydon CR0 4YY

CONTENTS

INTRODUCTION

Hello. I'm Glenn Murphy.

If you know my books at all, then you'll know that I'm no stranger to gross and icky things. I've written about the colour of **snot**, the loudness of **burps**, the power of **farts**, and more.

So when I set out to write this book, I had two new goals.

First, I would discover the most horrid, hideous and revolting things in the world and set about exploring the science behind them.

Second, I would try to gross *myself* out.

And do you know what? *I succeeded.*

As an author, a scientist and a reasonably tough guy, I thought I'd pretty much seen it all. But *nothing* could prepare me for **botflies**, **eye worms**, **scabies** or **casu marzu cheese** (just you wait).

2

So here we are. Ready to embark on an epic journey through the world of disgusting things. We'll meet **foul foods**, **beastly animals**, **yucky parasites** and **ghastly diseases**. Along the way, we'll meet **scientists** who study the most loathsome things you can imagine. And we'll be looking for answers to big and important **questions**, such as:

■ What is disgust, and what is it for?

■ Why are we disgusted by some things but not others?

■ Why are some people okay with some truly disgusting things?

Also, each chapter will begin with some questions for you – prompting you to examine and compare some disgusting things. You can discuss these questions with your friends, and even make a game out of it. (More about that on page 153).

I can't say for sure, but I'm betting that by the end of it all you'll find yourself a little **less** grossed out by things. Or at least, you'll understand **why** you find things disgusting, and how **useful** (or harmful) that response can be.

Ready to be grossed out?

Then let's go!

SMELLS A BIT OFF
The Science of Foul Food

Foul Foods from Around the World

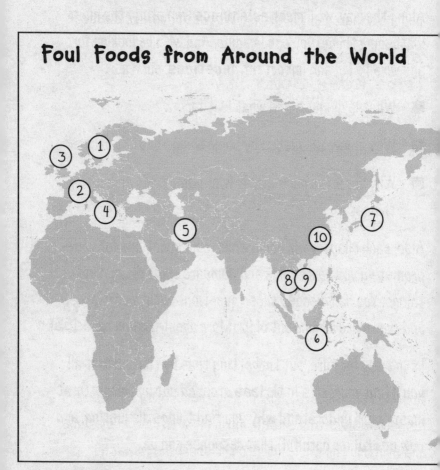

1) Sweden
Surströmming (sour herring)

Whitefish (typically Baltic herring) which is left to **rot** in barrels of salty water for up to **three months**, then **canned**.

Inside the can, bacteria **'ripen'** the fish, producing a sour flavour and an *awful* smell. So awful, in fact, that most people retch upon opening the can. Interestingly, fermented fish is also a key ingredient in British **Worcestershire sauce**.

2) France
Tripe (cow's stomach)

Tripe is eaten throughout the world but is especially popular in France. It is made from the **three-chambered stomach of a cow or pig** – steamed, boiled, or crammed into **Andouille sausages**. Oh là là!

3) Scotland
Haggis (sheep organs)

Scotland's national dish is made by mincing up the **heart, lungs and liver of a sheep**, mixing it with oats and onions, and stuffing the whole lot into the sheep's **stomach** (or, more commonly these days, into a **sausage casing**). The haggis is then boiled for several hours and served with 'neeps and tatties' (boiled turnips and potatoes). Mmmmm – boiled organ bag.

4) Sardinia
Casu Marzu (maggot cheese)

A cheese so disgusting it is illegal many countries. It is made by drilling a hole in a Pecorino cheese and encouraging cheese flies (*Piophila caseii*) to lay their eggs inside. The result is a sticky, gooey cheese swarming with hundreds of live, wriggling **maggots**, which leap off the cheese (and into your mouth) as you bite into it.

Pass the sickbag, please.

5) Iran
Kale Pache
(sheep's head)

A popular Middle-Eastern dish, also known as *khash*, made by **boiling the whole head of a sheep**, including the **brain**, **eyes** and **tongue**. In some places the **gooey, juicy eyeballs** are considered the best part, and are offered to honoured guests at the end of the meal.

Note to self: avoid being the honoured guest at a khash party.

6) Indonesia
Kopi Luwak (civet poo)

More an ingredient than a dish in itself, *kopi luwak* are coffee berries that have been (no joke) eaten, digested and plopped out by **palm civets** — small tree-dwelling mammals native to south-east Asia. The half-digested, poo-covered beans are then washed and used to make a rare and expensive coffee drink, of the same name. In other words, rich people pay big money to drink **liquefied, poo-tinged coffee**. This would be funny, if it wasn't so gross.

7) Japan
Hachinoko (bee larvae)

Fat pale larvae of the **Japanese black bee** or **paper wasp**. These are gathered from nests by smoking out the stinging drones, which are then fried or boiled in soy sauce, and canned. Sweet, but starchy. Crunchy on the outside, gooey in the middle. What could be more delicious than a spoonful of bee babies? Err ... pretty much anything.

8) Cambodia
A'ping (deep-fried tarantulas)

Exactly what it sounds like. **Fat hairy fang-faced spiders deep-fried in peanut oil**, and usually served in a spicy lime and pepper sauce. The crispy legs taste like

Yes — this is a giant dish of deep-fried tarantulas.

8

prawns. The bulbous body tastes like – well – a fat hairy spider that eats insects for a living. *Yum.*

9) Vietnam
Con Ran (snake meat)

In Vietnam and surrounding regions, jungle snakes are enjoyed in various appetizing ways. Their meaty muscles are **boiled**, **grilled** or **stir-fried**. Their skin and bones are crushed and used to make **snake soup** and **snake porridge**. **Snake blood** is served in small glasses and gulped down all in one go. And **snake hearts** are served warm, fresh and still beating.

10) China
White Jade (monkey brains)

Too horrible to describe. But here goes: **fresh warm monkey brains**. Usually cooked, but sometimes not. Raw monkey brains are **scooped straight from the skull with a teaspoon**. [Shudder]

Suddenly I feel like becoming a vegetarian . . .

What's for Dinner?

Would You Rather...

- Eat boiled pig's feet or boiled sheep's eyes?
- Eat a crunchy tarantula kebab or a plate of deep-fried cockroaches?
- Eat a bowl full of cooked agave worms or a single raw jellyfish?

Pig's feet. Sheep's eyes. Spiders. Beetles. Worms. Jellyfish. Around the world, people eat *all kinds* of things. Many of these, you might think, are pretty revolting.

But who gets to decide which foods are delicious and which are disgusting? For that matter, who's to say what *is* food and what *isn't*? In short . . .

Why do we eat some things, but not others?

The reason we eat food, of course, is to **build and power our bodies**. All food contains nutrients – **sugars**, **fats** and **proteins** — which our bodies extract and absorb during **digestion**. Once inside the bloodstream, the body can use these to build (or rebuild) organs and tissues. Or it can break them down further to release chemical energy. Energy that we need to power every cell in our bodies.

Without food and the energy it provides, we could not keep moving, thinking or breathing for long. In fact, just **three weeks** without food would be enough to put most of us in a coma. It is hardly surprising, then, that humans try to find food wherever we can . . .

Some people — stage performers and Indian yoga masters — have gone a lot longer than this. But three weeks is the average.

So why do we eat animals for food?

Not all of us do. Some people follow religions like Buddhism, that forbid their followers from eating animals. Other religions and customs allow the eating of *some* animals (like chickens) but *not others* (like pigs). And some people simply choose a veggie-based diet because they believe it to be healthier, or simply don't want to eat animals.

This is, of course, perfectly okay. If we eat enough of them, **fruits**, **grains**, **nuts**, **seeds** and **vegetables** can provide all the nutrients and energy we need. And long ago that's exactly how our prehistoric ancestors stayed alive. They gathered roots. They picked fruits and berries. They nibbled on nuts and seeds. They wandered far and wide, seeking munchable plants wherever they could find them. This is called **foraging**.

But here's the problem with foraging — it takes a *lot* of searching and gathering to fuel our bodies this way. Plants are typically low in **protein**. Which is a problem for us, as the human body needs *plenty* of protein in order to build — among other things — **muscles**, **brains** and **blood cells**. You *can* get enough protein by eating plants alone. It's just that you need to eat a *lot* of them.

Land animals – like **cows**, **sheep** and **pigs** – eat *huge* quantities of plants and store *huge* amounts of protein in their fleshy bodies.

Sea animals – like **fish**, **crabs** and **clams** – do the same. Because of this, animals contain far more protein than plants do. So eating animals is a good way of getting *lots* of protein all at once.

For at least 200,000 years that's exactly how our human ancestors lived. They were **hunter-gatherers**. They **hunted animals** and they **gathered plants**.

When food, fish or game became sparse in one area, they moved on to the next. Some hunting tribes **followed herds of land animals** across entire continents – across Africa, Europe, Asia and the Americas. Others **moved along the coast** and hopped between islands on rafts, fishing as they went. This took them from south-east Asia to Australia, New Zealand and the Pacific islands. We humans literally chased our food across the globe!

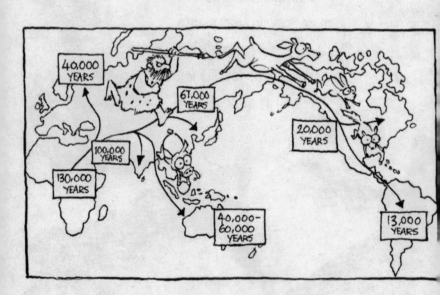

But that doesn't explain why we eat sheep and cows, but not, say, hippos and giraffes . . .

Well, around 10,000 years ago, a few bright sparks figured out that it would be *far* easier to *grow* and *keep* our food where we live than to spend all day hunting and foraging for it.

In the **Middle East**, **India** and parts of the **Americas**, people began growing **wheat**, **rice**, **corn** and **beans** in huge plots that could feed entire villages, or even *cities*. They also began *keeping* some of the animals they captured – typically the calm, slow-moving ones that were safe to live with. Then they started *breeding* them, to produce huge herds of edible animals. We call these **domestic animals**, or **livestock**.

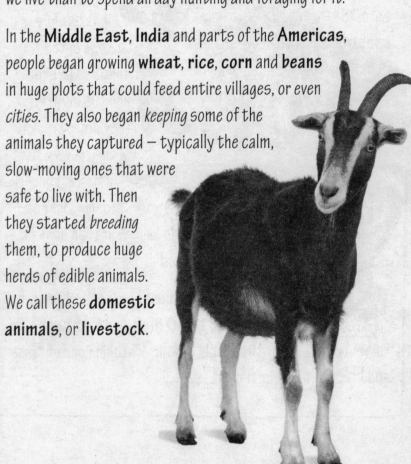

Since only **calm, safe** animals could be easily captured and domesticated (tamed), this ruled out many wild animals like **lions**, **leopards**, **hyenas**, **hippos** and **giraffes**.

You might not think **hippos** are that dangerous, but in fact, they are one of the most dangerous animals in Africa. They are extremely aggressive, have a fierce, bone-crushing bite and kill more people each year than lions or leopards combined!

Giraffes are no pushover either. They can sprint at up to **40 mph**, and have been known to kill a lion with a single kick. Try catching one of *those* and keeping it in your village!

But this 'calm + safe = delicious' rule still doesn't explain all of our animal food choices . . .

Look at it this way. **Zoologists** (scientists who study animal life) like to divide the animal kingdom into large groups, or **classes**. The six major classes of animals are **mammals**, **birds**, **reptiles**, **amphibians**, **fishes** and **invertebrates**.

Over the page is a short list of animals that we *commonly* eat (NOMZ) and *rarely* eat (NOPE).

ANIMAL CLASS	NOMZ	NOPE
mammals	cow	lion
	sheep	hippo
	goat	hyena
	llama	bear
	bison	wildebeest
	reindeer	dog
	yak	cat
	rabbit	rat
	guinea pig	porcupine
	kangaroo	platypus
	seal	walrus
birds	chicken	parrot
	turkey	wren
	goose	crow
	duck	owl
	quail	condor
	ostrich	puffin
	emu	penguin
reptiles	turtle	iguana
	crocodile	anaconda
	alligator	Komodo dragon

ANIMAL CLASS	NOMZ	NOPE
amphibians	edible frog bullfrog	newt salamander
fishes	cod carp trout salmon halibut grouper catfish European eel	triggerfish lionfish stonefish barracuda piranha angler fish tiger shark moray eel
invertebrates	snail clam oyster mussel lobster crab shrimp squid octopus	slug starfish flatworm cone shell centipede funnel-web spider barnacle box jelly coral

As you can see, people eat members of **every** animal class.

Granted, we eat some (fish, birds, mammals) more than others (amphibians, reptiles). And some of the animals in the NOMZ column may have surprised you. **Guinea pigs**, for example, aren't commonly eaten in Europe. But in parts of South America, they are common treats. Likewise, **snails**, **kangaroos** and **seals** aren't eaten often by the British or Americans. Yet they are savoured in parts of France, Australia and the Arctic.

In any case, this list shows us that humans will eat **all kinds** of animals. We are only picky about eating particular **species**.

So if it's not the kind of animal we're worried about, then what really decides which animal species are delicious and which are disgusting?

Let's see if we can come up with a few rules to help us decide . . .

Rule 1: Food should not be ferocious

Animals that are easily captured, kept and tamed make generally safe, convenient foods. Ferocious animals, on the other hand, do not. Among mammals, this rules out large **carnivores**, like **lions**, **bears** and **walruses**. For all we know, they might be *delicious* to eat. But to find out, we'd have to get past their claws, teeth and tusks. So we tend to avoid them and eat tamer, less ferocious things instead.

Exceptions

Crocodile and **alligator**. Both are farmed and eaten in Africa and parts of the southern United States. In Florida and Georgia, barbecued 'gator is served smothered in sweet tangy sauce, and deep-fried 'gator bites' are served as an appetizer. They taste a bit like tough chewy chicken.

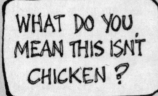

Rule 2: Food should not be poisonous

This is one is pretty obvious. If eating an animal makes you sick or kills you, then you probably shouldn't do it. Among amphibians, this puts the **edible frog** on the menu, but removes other, toxic, frog species, and most **newts** and **salamanders**. Although many of these would be safe to eat, we tend to avoid the whole animal family, since safe salamanders and toxic salamanders can be hard to tell apart.

Exceptions

Fugu and **snails**. Fugu (pufferfish) contains a potent poison called tetrodotoxin, which causes paralysis and death. Yet it is prepared and eaten in expensive restaurants across Japan and Korea. Specially trained chefs take great care to remove the poisonous liver, ovaries and intestines before cooking the fish. This prevents the deadly toxin from leaking into the flesh. Most of the time. Similarly, snails are eaten in many parts of Europe and Africa. But slugs are generally avoided, as they cover themselves in a thick toxic slime to deter predators – including us.

Rule 3: Food should not be venomous

This ties in with Rule 1. An animal may be perfectly safe to eat once captured. But if it can kill you with a single bite or sting, then you'd be better off not trying to capture it. This puts the **common squid** and **oyster** on the menu, but rules out the **blue-ringed octopus** and **cone shell**. All of these are in the same animal family (**molluscs**). But while the first two species are harmless, the other two have venomous bites or stings that can kill you in under a minute. This is how nature says 'nope'.

Exceptions

Cobras and **rattlesnakes**. Although venomous, neither of these snakes are poisonous to eat. And if you know how to catch and handle them (typically their heads are held down using special hooked sticks, then they're stuffed into drawstring bags), then hunting snakes is worth the risk. Venomous snakes are eaten throughout China, India and South America.

Get It Sorted: Venomous and Poisonous – What's the Difference?

If something is venomous or poisonous, it means it is toxic and if you come into contact with it, it could make you very ill, or possibly even kill you. The difference between the two is the way that the toxin is delivered. Venom is manufactured by an organism in a gland and then pumped into its prey/attacker using some kind of specialized delivery system, such as a fang or stinger.

If something is poisonous on the other hand, it doesn't deliver its toxin directly. Instead, its whole body, or large parts of it, may contain the poisonous substance. So while a frog or a mushroom may not look dangerous, it may contain a toxin that makes you very ill if you touch or ingest it.

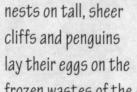

Rule 4: Food should not be impossible to catch

Some animals, while perfectly edible and not particularly ferocious, are just too hard to find or capture. Chickens roost on the ground. But puffins make their nests on tall, sheer cliffs and penguins lay their eggs on the frozen wastes of the Antarctic.

Puffins have been eaten in food-poor places where other food is even harder to catch, and are still eaten in Iceland. And Antarctic explorers sometimes ate penguin in desperation – but apparently it tastes horrible.

Hence, we eat chickens and chicken eggs, but *rarely* puffins, penguins, or the eggs of either one.

The same goes for **pelagic squid** versus **colossal squid**. Small, **pelagic squid** live in shallow water close to shore and are easily caught. **Colossal squid** grow up to **14 metres** in length and weigh up to **half a tonne**. If you caught one and kept it frozen, you could probably live off it for four or five years. But colossal squid are rarely ever caught. This is because they live at incredible depths, in freezing waters beyond the reach of our nets. Too tough to catch, and therefore off the menu.

Exceptions
Whales are too large to hunt with conventional hooks and nets. They, too, live in deep waters, and can remain submerged for long periods to avoid capture. Yet sadly, they are still hunted by whaling boats armed with high-tech radar and explosive harpoons. Whale is still widely eaten in Japan, Norway, Iceland and Greenland.

Rule 5: Food should not be cute

Cats, **dogs**, **hamsters**, **monkeys**, **parrots** and **dolphins** are all, in theory, edible. They are not especially ferocious. They are not poisonous or venomous. And being friendly animals, they are not particularly difficult to catch. So why do we avoid scoffing them?

The simple answer is because they look cute, they give us loyalty and affection, and (unless we are starving to death) we enjoy looking after them more than we do eating them.

Domestic animals like these also serve other purposes around the house, making them more useful as **pets** than as **dinner**.

The word 'domestic' comes from the Latin word *domus*, meaning 'home'. **Domestic dogs** make good pets, guards and hunting pals. **Domestic cats** keep your house rodent-free (if a little hairy). And before the advent of cars, trains and planes, domesticated **horses** were the fastest way to get around.

Exceptions

Pretty much every cute animal on the planet. At one time or another, **cats**, **dogs**, **hamsters**, **monkeys**, **parrots**, **dolphins** and all manner of other cute animals have all been hunted and eaten by humans. In many places, they still are . . .

So what have we learned?

First, that we avoid eating *some* animals for **safety** reasons – to avoid being **injured** or **poisoned**. This is why we don't *generally* eat **slugs**, **scorpions** or **hyenas**. And we find the idea of eating them disgusting.

Second, we avoid eating some animals because we **connect** with them. This is why we don't eat generally eat **cats**, **beagles** or **marmosets**. We feel bad about eating a cute, furry pal, and find the idea of doing so disgusting.

Third – which animals we connect with depends upon the **customs** of the communities we live in. Guinea pigs are pets in Britain, where the idea of eating them is horrible. But in the South American Andes guinea pigs aren't pets, they're lunch. Elsewhere in the world, the same goes for **monkeys**, **horses**, **dolphins** and **whales**.

This also tells us that ideas of **disgust** are not *shared* by everyone. They are *learned*.

Finally – if you're desperate or hungry enough, there's no such thing as a 'disgusting food'.

Well, almost . . .

Smelly, Mouldy and Rotten

Would You Rather…

- Eat a year-old rotten egg or a can of stinky rotten whitefish?
- Eat a plate of mouldy beans or a slice of maggot-ridden cheese?
- Drink a pint of sour horse's milk or a cup of sour human spit?

If there's one thing that seems to turn **everybody's** stomach, it's the thought of eating **rotten, mouldy food**. The very sight of a mouldy peach can make us retch. And the smell of sour milk and rotten eggs can make us vomit.

And for good reason. Rotten foods are often swarming with harmful **bacteria**, and the **fungi** growing on mouldy fruit contain **toxins** that can damage our delicate stomachs. Eating too much of either can lead to nasty (perhaps even deadly) bouts of **food poisoning**.

So our disgust at rotten, mouldy things is a form of **self-defence**. We shun rotten eggs, mouldy fruit and sour-smelling milk and meat because our ancestors learned – long,

long ago — that these things can be **harmful to our bodies**. The ones who **didn't** learn that lesson rarely survived long enough to have children, so aren't among our ancestors.

How, then, do some people cheerily gulp down sour milk and mouldy-seaweed tea?

Or chomp their way through heaps of year-old cheese and cabbage? Put another way . . .

Why do we eat mouldy old cheese, but not mouldy old fruit and vegetables?

Cheese is made and eaten throughout the world but is particularly popular in Europe. English **Cheddar**, French **Brie**, Italian **mozzarella**, Greek **feta** . . . the list goes on and on. No **pizza**, **lasagne** or **toastie** would be complete without it. Sometimes we eat great *chunks* of cheese for dessert, all on its own.

But if you think about **what cheese really is**, it could considered a pretty disgusting thing to eat. If an alien landed tomorrow, and asked you about the cheese sandwich you were eating, the conversation might go a little like this...

Alien: Greetings, earthling. What are you eating there?

You: Er . . . a cheese sandwich. You've never seen a cheese sandwich?

Alien: No. What is it?

You: A slice of cheese, between two slices of bread.

Alien: I see. And how do you make this 'bread'?

You: You add yeast to crushed plant grains, warm the mixture it until it rises, then cut it into slices.

Alien: What is 'yeast'?

You: A kind of fungus that grows on sugary things.

Alien: I see. And the cheese?

You: You add bacteria to cow's milk, which makes it curdle. Then you pick out the solid lumps, squeeze out the water and leave the lumps to ripen for a few months. Or maybe a few years.

Alien: So let me get this straight – you're eating year-old chunks of cow juice, pressed between slices of baked fungus-grains?

You: Er . . . I suppose so, yes.

Alien: Thank you. We're off to find a less disgusting planet.
Farewell, gross-lings.

Other potentially revolting European foodstuffs include bacteria-ripened milk (**yoghurt**), mouldy grape juice (**wine**) and mouldy grain juice (**beer**).

Beyond mainland Europe, we find mouldy soya beans (**Japanese natto**), rotten cabbage (**Korean kimchi**), rotten shark-meat (**Icelandic hakari**) and drinks made from boiled corn left to rot in human saliva (**Ecuadorian chicha**).

All these foods have one thing in common. They are made by encouraging the growth of *some* types of bacteria (or fungus), but *not others*.

Food left to rot in a warm environment will be colonized by **microbes** (microscopic **bacteria** or **fungi**) within hours. These tiny organisms break down (or rot) our food, and many produce harmful chemicals as they grow.

This is why we keep foods **chilled**, **frozen** and **sealed off** in airtight containers. Packaging helps keep the fungal and bacterial spores off the food in the first place, and low temperatures slow their growth.

But **fermented foods** – like **yoghurt**, **beer** and **kimchi** – are made by encouraging the growth of some microbes, but not others. Fermented foods are made using safe, healthy microbes that feed on sweet sugars and convert them into sour-tasting acids.

These acids prevent the growth of nasty, harmful microbes, and make these 'rotten' foods safe to eat. In fact, many fermented foods are considered very healthy, as they transfer helpful 'good' bacteria to our intestines, where they help keep out harmful bacteria.

The acids also add a sour taste to fermented foods, which some people love, and others loathe. This is why most Europeans love cheese, but few can stomach *natto* (fermented soy beans). On the flipside, many Japanese people love *natto*, but consider cheese (especially soft or blue cheese) pretty disgusting. It all depends where you grow up and what you get used to.

But let's face it – no one outside Ecuador likes drinks made from corn and human spit. Urgh!

Waste Not, Want Not

Would You Rather...

- Eat a bull's tongue or a bowlful of pig's guts?
- Slurp down a live oyster or a bowl of snake-blood soup?
- Eat a slimy sea urchin or a whole squirming octopus?

These days, when people talk about 'meat' in their diet, they usually mean one of the following things:

- whole chunks of muscle from livestock (**beef**, **lamb**)
- fatty, minced muscle with bits of bone and cartilage, also from livestock (**minced beef or lamb**)
- muscle from the breast, thigh or hindquarters of a chicken (**chicken breasts**, **thighs** or **drumsticks**).

Some people vary this, of course, adding more exotic meats like **goose**, **duck**, **quail**, **ostrich** or **bison**. But even then, they're still eating the tender, lean **muscles** of the **bird** or **mammal** in question.

This is perhaps surprising, since the word 'meat' means:

> 'the edible part of a fruit, nut or animal, as opposed to its covering (husk, shell or bones)'

So the meat of a **coconut** or **peanut** includes **everything but its shell**. **Crab meat** and **oyster meat** are defined the same way. When it comes to animal meats, then . . .

Why do we eat some parts of an animal but not others?

More specifically, why do we only eat the **muscles** of all those **edible birds and mammals**? Surely there are plenty of other edible bits that we're missing . . .

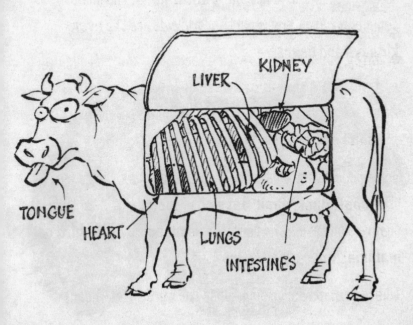

TONGUE

HEART

LIVER

KIDNEY

LUNGS

INTESTINES

Well, the simple answer is, there *are* other edible bits. Tasty ones too. These rarer, non-muscular cuts are called **organ meats** or **offal** (not to be confused with '**awful**').

Now here's the funny thing about organ meats. While most modern British, North American and Australian diners avoid them, organ meats are *extremely* popular throughout the rest of the world.

In fact, up until the mid-twentieth century, organ meats were also highly prized in Britain and America (your nan and grandad probably ate them and loved them)! Back then, the organs were considered the **tastiest part** of the animal — as they still are in other parts of the world. The most commonly eaten 'spare parts' worldwide are the **liver**, **kidneys** and **heart**.

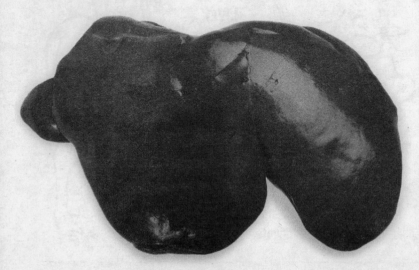

At first glance, eating slimy animal organs might seem pretty gross. But if you think about it, why *shouldn't* we eat them? After all, these organs are actually much richer in important **nutrients** than simple muscle tissue. These include **vitamins**, **minerals**, and **essential fatty acids**.

One of the jobs of the **liver** is to store vitamins – complex chemicals that are essential for good health. A good slab of liver contains healthy doses of **vitamins A, B, D, E** and **K**. Organ meats also contain **essential minerals** – like calcium, iron, potassium, selenium and magnesium – which *are* present in muscle meat, but in much lower amounts.

So if you can stomach them, it might be worth popping a few of these in your gob from time to time . . .

Top 10 Most Popular Types of Offal and Organ Meat

1 **Liver** – Cow, pig, lamb, chicken, goose and fish livers are eaten worldwide. In the UK, liver is served fried, with onions. In France, pork and goose livers are minced to make **pâtés.**

2 **Kidneys** – Served in traditional British **steak-and-kidney pies**, or spiced up and slopped on to a slice of bread for **devilled kidneys on toast.**

3 **Tongue** – Fatty **beef tongue** is popular throughout Europe, China and the Middle East. In the UK, it is minced up with liver and breadcrumbs to make **faggots.**

4 **Feet –** Pig's or lamb's feet are a popular delicacy in Asia, but are also found in many French, German and Irish recipes. And before you turn your nose up, the jelly in British pork pies comes from boiled feet too.

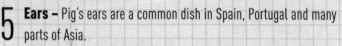

5 **Ears –** Pig's ears are a common dish in Spain, Portugal and many parts of Asia.

6 **Intestines – Pig** and **sheep intestines** are eaten everywhere from Europe to Africa, Asia and the Americas. In Turkey and Greece, **lamb intestines** are served grilled on a spit. In Korea and China, **pig's guts** are added to stews. Old English recipes called them *chitterlings*. In the southern United States, **boiled** or **deep-fried hog's guts** are still known as '*chitlins'*.

7 **Heart – Beef heart** is found on menus across Eastern Europe and is especially popular in Russia. **Horse hearts** often make a 'hearty' meal in Mongolia.

8 **Lungs –** Lungs are used in **sausages** worldwide, and sometimes chopped and added to **minced beef** to give it a more 'airy' texture.

9 **Bone Marrow – Marrow** is a rubbery foodstuff removed from the middle of backbones and leg bones. It is often poached and served on toast, or as a meal in itself. It is very popular in Lebanese dishes.

10 **Blood Sausage –** Also known as **blood pudding**, or black pudding, blood sausage is made by shaping l**umps of congealed blood** into sausages or pancakes and frying them. It's found throughout Europe, Asia and Africa, and a prized ingredient in the traditional full English breakfast.

Of course, eating a **cooked** heart or blood sausage is a lot easier than eating a **raw** one.

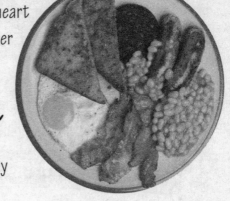

That would just be disgusting, right?

Well, maybe, maybe not. In any case, it's worth asking . . .

Why do we bother to cook our food, when other animals eat things raw?

Most animals eat their food **raw**, or **still wriggling**. And for most of the history of our species, we humans did too.

Humans are the only creatures on the planet that **cook their food**. You don't see **lizards** roasting insects on hot stones before they chomp into them . . . **bears** blackening their salmon on a stick . . . or a pride of **lions** grilling a fresh-caught antelope . . . you get the idea.

PUFF! PUFF!

In the entire animal kingdom, only humans bother to **boil**, **roast**, **fry** and **grill** their food. So why go to all this trouble? What's the point?

As you may have guessed, there is more than one answer to this question. Here are a few points you might consider:

Animals are rubbish at making fires

'Animals cooking things?' you might say. *'That's just daft! Lizards, bears and lions don't have thumbs and can't grip sticks or tongs. So how could they roast or grill things without burning themselves?'*

Fair point. But even within the thumb-bearing **Primate** family to which our species belongs, you don't see much cooking going on. **Lemurs**, **monkeys**, **gorillas**, **chimpanzees** . . . all of these animals have been known to use tools — wielding long sticks to retrieve out-of-reach fruit, or stones to crack tough nutshells. But do they spear their food with sticks and hold it over a fire? No.

WANT ME TO THROW ANOTHER RABBIT ON THE BARBIE?

'*That's cos they're scared of fire,*' you might argue.

Fair enough. But you don't necessarily need fire to cook food. Under a blazing sun, desert rocks heat up to oven-like temperatures. Yet no animal uses those to roast their prey.

And every winter, on the snow-covered island of Hokkaido, **Japanese macaques**, also known as **snow monkeys**, sit in **boiling natural spring waters** (or *onsen*) to relax and warm up. But do they boil their mushrooms, insects and plant roots in the hot springs before scoffing them? No. And there's no reason to believe they ever will.

Cooking food makes it easier to eat

Now *this* sounds a bit more likely. Most **carnivores** – like **cats** and **dogs** – have sharp canine teeth for tearing at their meat, and strong stomachs that can tolerate half-rotten scraps. **Herbivores** – like **sheep** and **horses** – have tough, flat molars for chewing seeds, grasses and woody stems, and their stomachs contain bacteria that break down tough plant tissues.

But compared to most other animals, humans have **weak jaws**, **brittle teeth** and **weak stomachs**. So one reason we roast, boil and bake our meat and vegetables is to **soften them up**, making them easier to chew and digest.

Cooking food makes it safer and healthier to eat

Heating can destroy some **vitamins** and **nutrients** stored in raw meat and vegetables. But it also kills the **harmful bacteria** and **parasites** that lurk within.

Fruits and **veggies** start decaying the moment they are picked or uprooted, and the bacteria they harbour can make

us ill. But they stay fresh for a good while, and even *rotten* veg will rarely cause anything worse than a stomach ache.

This is not so for animal-based foods. Most **fish** and **shellfish** can be safely eaten raw, provided that they're scoffed right away. This is how we get away with eating **raw oysters** and Japanese-style **raw fish** (*sushi* and *sashimi*) on a regular basis.

But some raw seafood can contain harmful bacteria, or tiny parasitic roundworms called **nematodes** (more about these later). Eating uncooked tuna or oysters with *those* bad boys inside could make you very sick indeed.

NEMATODES?

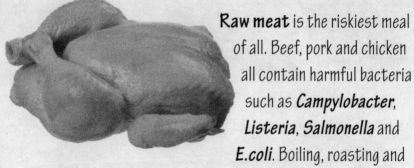

Raw meat is the riskiest meal of all. Beef, pork and chicken all contain harmful bacteria such as **Campylobacter**, **Listeria**, **Salmonella** and **E.coli**. Boiling, roasting and grilling will destroy all of these (provided that the meat is heated right through so no 'cold spots' remain within).

That said, raw meats **are** still eaten worldwide. In Japan, **namatori** (raw chicken chunks) and **shabu-shabu** (raw beef slices) are served over bowls of cooked rice, and rarely make people ill, provided that the meat is *very* fresh.

Some even go beyond raw food, and eat *live* animals too. You can't get much fresher than that, I guess . . .

Top 5 Eaten-Alive Dishes, Worldwide

Raw Oysters (Europe)

Oysters are most often served alive in their shells. Diners squeeze on a little lemon (which makes the oyster shrink and recoil) before tipping the slithering *living* creature straight down their throats. *Bleurgh.*

Drunken Shrimp (China)

Live shrimp, served swimming drunkenly in a large bowl of white wine.

Ikizukuri (Japan)

Chunks of *sashimi* carved from an unfortunate living fish, squid or lobster, and served on a plate with the rest of its still-twitching body.

Sannakji (Korea)

Freshly chopped live octopuses in a bowl. Lopping off the tentacles does not kill them right away. So they often flee the plate (or crawl off the dinner table) soon after they are served.

Sawagani (Japan)

Tiny freshwater river crabs served alive and eaten whole. Sometimes these crabs contain a parasitic flatworm (or lung fluke) called *Paragonimus westermani*. Eating an infected crab transfers the worm to your bloodstream. From there, it may travel to the lungs and multiply – collapsing your lungs and possibly killing you.

Which, some might say, would probably serve you right . . .

Icky Science
Expert 1

I study the things that make people sick.

Dr Benjamin Chapman, North Carolina State University

What's your job title and what do you study?

Assistant Professor, Food Safety Extension Specialist. I research food safety from farm to fork with an emphasis on bacteria and viruses. It's called **risk analysis**, basically investigating everything around food-borne illnesses like food poisoning. Stuff like how much hand-washing and cross-contamination happens in restaurant kitchens and what people do with food in their homes. I work to help farmers, grocery stores, restaurants and regular people to keep food safe.

How does your job help benefit the world?

My work reveals more about the food system and gives us a better understanding of risks to the food supply. More (and better) data on how food is handled can lead to better solutions on keeping food safe.

What got you interested in science?

The idea that there are a lot of things we don't know a lot about – and that with each discovery we make, we can advance science. I got really interested in things that make people sick back when I was in high school. Viruses in particular – the idea that something so, *so* small can invade a body and use the host's cells to make more of themselves – is just an amazing thing.

What's the most disgusting thing you've ever seen or done in connection with your job?

I fell into a pond that was full of manure as I was trying to get a water sample.

FILTHY CRITTERS AND CREEPY-CRAWLIES

The Science of Revolting Animals

Would You Rather...

- Hug a hairy pig or cuddle a slimy octopus?
- Handle a scuttling centipede or grab a slippery eel?
- Have a worm on your chin or a beetle in your ear?

What makes a revolting animal?

This might seem like a pretty simple question. But it's a tricky one to answer.

After all, not everyone is disgusted by the *same* things, are they?

As a rule, city dwellers can't stand **rats**, **mice** and **cockroaches**. Yet country folk are fine with them. A **slug** found in a supermarket will make shoppers shriek.

But gardeners pick them off their lettuces with a shrug. And while *most* people flinch at the thought of a **spider** or **centipede** scuttling across their skin, some really aren't bothered by this thought at all.

What makes some animals so disgusting, while others seem likable or even lovable?

The Aliens Are Coming!

One simple answer to that question is this: **we tend to fear and loathe things that are alien to us**.

As we learned in the last chapter, weird foods disgust us largely because they are strange (or unknown) to us. Well, the same goes for strange or odd-looking animals.

In short, humans tend to like being around animals that **look**, **feel** and **behave much like us**.

The animals we keep as friends and companions (**cats**, **dogs**, **rabbits**, **hamsters**, **horses**, **monkeys**) are mostly **mammals**. These are all **hairy** or **furry** animals with **two eyes**, **two ears**, **one mouth** and a recognizable 'head' end and '**tail' end**. They walk, hop or scamper, on **two** or **four legs**, in reassuringly familiar ways.

On the flipside, the animals we tend to avoid — and find revolting — are those **least like us**.

Worms, **snakes**, **frogs**, **spiders** and **insects** are all from different animal classes to our own. Their strange, alien body shapes scare us. Their **hairless**, **scaly** or **slimy skins**

feel odd to the touch. And their **scuttling**, **slithering** and **creeping** movements bother us.

In between these two extremes — animals very **like** us, and animals very **unlike** us — lie all the rest. In other words animals we find neither cute nor disgusting.

For the most part, these are wild mammals that are less familiar to us, but not strange enough to freak us out. At a pinch, we might *eat* them. But most of us won't be inviting them into our homes any time soon. These 'in-betweeners' include **tapirs**, **llamas**, **weasels**, **wolverines**, **marmots**, **sloths**, **anteaters** and many, many more.

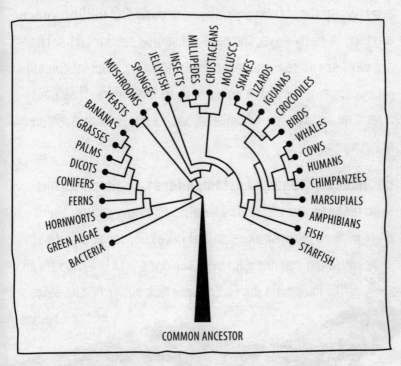

COMMON ANCESTOR

Generally speaking, the **further** from us an animal is on the evolutionary tree, the **more likely** we are to find it disgusting. I call this the '**disgusting alien**' rule.

Let's look at a few examples...

Alien Reptiles and Amphibians

In truth, reptiles and amphibians aren't so far removed from us mammals.

Mammals evolved from mammal-like reptiles during the **Triassic Age**, around **250 million** years ago, while **reptiles** probably split off from amphibians around **60 million years earlier**. In many ways, they are still quite similar to us. They are **vertebrates** — meaning that they have a spinal column (or backbone). They have no more than four limbs. They have a recognizable head and tail end, with a single body section in between.

But **lizards**, **frogs** and **salamanders** lack our plush, furry skin. Instead, they have **dry scales** or **slimy skins**. The ones with no legs (**snakes** and **skinks**) slither and writhe in a creepy, alien manner. And even the ones *with* legs don't walk like mammals do. Their legs stick out from the sides of their bodies,

rather than prop them up from beneath. So they **creep** and **crawl** around on their bellies, as if they're always sneaking up on someone.

Of course, some people *love* amphibians and reptiles. They keep **tree frogs**, **tree pythons** and **leopard geckos** in heated glass tanks, feed them crickets and mice and handle them while they watch TV. But for every snake-loving human out there, there are at least two who would really rather not touch them at all.

Alien Bugs and Spiders

Insects and **spiders** are almost twice as old as mammals, having first appeared on our planet during the **Devonian period**, about **400 million** years ago. They belong to a larger family of animals called **arthropods**, and they are almost *nothing* like us.

For starters, they are **invertebrates** — meaning that they have **no backbone or internal skeleton**. Instead, they wear

Thorax

Abdomen

Exoskeleton

their skeletons on the **outside** – in the form of a hard, brittle **exoskeleton** or **carapace**.

Insects have six legs, while **spiders** have eight, and other arthropods have **10**, **12** or even **50** or more. While they do generally have a clear head and tail end, their bodies are divided into two sections or **segments** – an upper segment called the **thorax**, and a lower segment called the **abdomen**.

Because of this, insects and spiders not only *look* very different to mammals, they *move* very differently too. They use their multiple legs to **step**, **scuttle**, **jump** and **crawl** – often in sudden, erratic ways. Some insects – like **flies**, **beetles** and **mosquitoes** – buzz around us on thrumming, paper-thin wings, threatening to bite us, sting us, or buzz right into our faces.

To make matters worse, many also have terrifying **jaws**, **pincers** and **mandibles**, and weird-looking **antennae** that stick out of their alien heads! Most insects and spiders are too small to see in detail. But the bigger they are, the more terrifyingly alien they appear.

Underwater Aliens

Fish and sea creatures aren't disgusting by default, of course. But some aquatic animals are more weird-looking than others, and it's *these* species that tend to gross us out.

Like us, fish are **vertebrates** with recognizable heads, tails, eyes and mouths. So far, so good. But fish with odd-shaped bodies, eyes or mouths tend *not* to appear in our home aquariums. Don't believe me? Just compare the cute, patterned face of the **clownfish** to the terrifying gape of the **anglerfish**. Or the plump, majestic **koi carp** found in

ponds across the world to the slimy, wriggling **eels** of the open oceans.

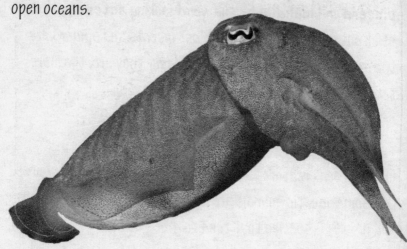

Other 'underwater aliens' include **octopuses**, **cuttlefish**, **jellyfish** and **sea slugs**. How gross we find *these* might well depend on how close we get to them. From a distance, their alien shapes and colourful **skins** can be quite beautiful. But few of us enjoy the thought of their wet, slimy bodies pressed against our bare skin.

Some squid, octopus and cuttlefish species actually communicate with each other, using patterns of coloured light on their skin, like living TV screens! For more on this, see my animal science book, Evolution, Nature and Stuff.

You Make Me Sick!

Would You Rather...

- Kiss a frog or lick a toad?
- Be caressed by a python or surrounded by hornets?
- Be stung by a jellyfish or bitten by a tarantula?

For many people, **snakes**, **spiders** and **slimy amphibians** (frogs, toads and salamanders) are in a revolting class all of their own.

Mice and cockroaches might give you the creeps. But the thought of holding a **fat, slimy frog** – or a **wriggling, hairy spider** – might make you want to throw up!

The funny thing is, young **children** are often **fine** with picking up these animals, but **adults** are **not**. Why is that?

Granted, **spiders**, **snakes** and **frogs** look pretty different from us. So they could easily fall into the 'disgusting aliens' category. But then why would kids be *fine* with them, while adults are totally *grossed out*?

Once again, this is largely about **fear**. As we've already learned, humans tend to fear things that are strange or unknown to us. But snakes, spiders and slimy things are especially scary (and therefore disgusting) because they are not only **strange**, but also **dangerous**. Or so we think . . .

Frogs, **toads** and **salamanders** are slimy because their skins are covered with a protective goo, which helps keep them moist when they are out of the water. This slime oozes out of special glands in the skin. In *some* frog species – and especially toads – this slime is **foul-tasting** or **poisonous**. This helps to deter predators like snakes and birds.

All toads are frogs, but only some frogs are toads. 'Toad' is a name given to certain frog species – usually with bumpy, warty skin, covered in toxic slime.

At some point, our human ancestors hunted and **ate** frogs, and those that survived figured out that many of the slimy ones were poisonous. Therefore, our disgust at eating slimy frogs and toads probably developed as a protection against poisoning.

But here's the thing – there are over **3,000 species of frog, toad and salamander** on the planet. Of these, **less than 300** could be be toxic. So its a case of 'Better safe than sorry'.

Yeah, but surely most snakes and spiders are poisonous?

Nope! Neither of these animal families are poisonous – meaning that if you really wanted to, you could eat them without getting sick. But some of them do have a **venomous bite**.

Of the world's **2,700** known snake species, around **400** are considered dangerous to humans. These include many species of rattlesnake and viper, and the deadly **black mamba**, **Philippine cobra**, **blue krait** and **taipan**. Some of these snakes can kill with a single bite, with venoms that clot your blood, liquefy your organs or paralyse your heart and lungs. Krait bites kill within hours, black mamba bites within minutes. Little wonder, then, that we should be so fearful of (and disgusted by) slithering snakes.

No one knows for sure how many **spider** species there are. It could be anywhere from 10,000 to 100,000. All spiders have a paralysing venom. Some – like the **black widow**, **funnel-web spider**, and **Brazilian wandering spider** – have bites

Black widow

than can kill an adult human within hours. Again – little wonder that we fear their little scuttling shapes.

But in fact, more than **85 per cent of the world's snakes** – and more than **99 per cent of its spiders** – are **completely harmless**. So just like slimy frogs and toads, they get a bad rap. Although only a **few** of them are genuinely dodgy, we've learn to be afraid of (and revolted by) them **all**.

This partly explains why *most* people are disgusted by them, but others (including children) are *not*. We have an inborn **suspicion** of snakes, spiders and slimy frogs which has helped keep us alive since the beginning of human history. But for those of us who get to *know* these animals – catching frogs in the local pond as children, or keeping non-venomous snakes and spiders as pets – they no longer hold any fear. So there's no reason to be disgusted by them.

Interestingly, in places like **Papua New Guinea**, where humans still hunt frogs, snakes and spiders for food, **no one** is disgusted by them. Local tribes might consider certain species **delicious** or **dangerous**. But never *disgusting*. They're just another part of the scenery.

Which just goes to show you once more – disgust is both **learned and unlearned**.

Icky Science Expert 2

I study the things that live in your belly button.

Dr Rob Dunn, North Carolina State University

What's your job title and what do you study?

I'm an Assistant Professor of Biology and science writer, based at North Carolina State University. In short, I study the things that live in, on and around humans. This includes bacteria in your belly button, mites on your head and all of those things that crawl under your bed.

Why? How does your job help benefit the world?

Most of the animals in the world have never been studied. This is true of the rainforest. It is true in your house. My job is to study some of these species so we can begin to understand what they do, which are good or bad and how it is that they came to live alongside us in the first place. Some of the species in your house might save your life one day; some might make you sick, but first we have to know who and what they are.

What first got you interested in science?

When I was a kid I spent all my time outside poking at things and trying to understand the life around me. At some point I realized that many of the things I didn't know about as a kid no one knows about. That realization was and continues to be fantastic to me. More is unknown about the world than known.

What's the most disgusting thing you've ever seen or done in connection with your job?

Ha! Well, insects aren't really so disgusting. Neither are bacteria. Sometimes people are disgusting though. We once did a project where we tried to trap insects on Broadway in Manhattan, New York City. The *insects* behaved well. But the *people* . . . well . . . some of them peed in our traps.

Filthy Habits

Would You Rather...

- Cover yourself in snot or roll in diarrhoea?
- Be sprayed with pee or squirted with vomit?
- Drink your own drool or eat your own poo?

So the 'disgusting alien' theory explains why we prefer furry mammals over scaly reptiles and scuttling spiders.

But it doesn't explain everything about which animals we find disgusting. Otherwise, why would we prefer **hamsters** over **rats**, **cats** over **skunks**, or **parrots** over **vultures**?

Within these three pairings, each animal looks much like the other. The first pair are **rodents**, the second **carnivores**, and the third **birds**. So why do so few of us keep pet rats, pet skunks and pet vultures?

*Yeah, yeah – I **know** some of you readers have pet rats. I'm sure they're lovely. But given the choice of pet rodent, at least ten times more of you went for gerbils, hamsters or guinea pigs instead. So while not **everyone** thinks they're disgusting, rats are clearly far less popular.*

The answer is that they *look* the same, but they *behave* quite differently. Humans generally aren't fond of **animals with filthy habits**. Specifically, habits that have to do with **blood**, **urine** or **faeces** (poo).

What do you mean, 'filthy habits'?

Many **insects** eat, lay their eggs in or otherwise live on poo. **Dung beetles** are famously fond of poo, getting almost all of their nutrition from the gooey dung of herbivores. Some roll balls of dung into their nests to feed themselves and their young. Others bury dung-balls underground to keep them 'fresh' and lay their eggs on top. And some species simply set up shop in fresh dung piles — moving in for as long as it takes for them to chew through their poo-based houses.

This seems to work well for them. As insects go, dung beetles are spectacularly successful. They are found on every continent except Antarctica, where there are no native herbivores to provide fresh food and housing. (I guess frozen penguin poo doesn't quite make the grade.) But poo-eating is common among other insects too — including **houseflies**, **dragonflies**, **butterflies** and **termites**.

Beyond the insect family, **cats**, **dogs**, **pigs**, **cows**, **rabbits**, **pandas** and **elephants** all like to indulge in a little poop-scoffing too.

Why would any animal want to eat its own poo?

They do this for a variety of reasons. **Rabbits** eat their poo (the scientific name for this is *coprophagy*) in order to digest their food better. Unlike cows and sheep, they lack the multi-chambered stomachs needed to digest the tough woody plants and grasses they nibble on. So after passing a ball of food through their guts, they plop it out, pop the droppings back in their mouth and give it a second or third pass. Those bunnies don't seem quite so cuddly now, do they?

Young **elephants** and **hippos** eat poo for another reason. They pluck it from their mother's bottoms in order to fill their guts with bacteria. Without these gut-bugs, the young animals would be unable to digest the leaves and grasses their parents eat.

Closer to our own animal family, **gorillas** and **chimpanzees** eat their own (and each other's) faeces too. We don't know whether this is for extra digestion, extra vitamins or just for fun. But in any case, it *is* pretty disgusting.

Besides the **poo-eaters**, we also tend to dislike **sprayers**, **spitters** and **pukers**. These are animals that spray their own **poo**, **urine**, **vomit** and even **blood** at predators as a means of self-defence. This tactic is used by several fish, frog and mammal species, but is more common in **reptiles** and **birds**. (Since birds evolved from reptiles, this is not so surprising.) For a sampling of truly of revolting animal habits, feast your eyes on the following list . . .

Top 10 Filthy Animal Habits

1 Puke Spray – **Fulmars** ('foul-gulls') are gull-like seabirds that live on rocky cliffs throughout the Atlantic and Pacific. When threatened, fulmar babies spray predators (or unlucky rock climbers) full in the face with a jet of foul-smelling fishy orange vomit.

2 Pee Spray – The football-sized **desert tortoise** stores up to a litre (two pints) of water in its body. Give it a scare, and it'll spray most of that into your face, all at once, like a high-pressure fire hose.

3 Poo Spray – The **hoopoe** is a large bird of the kingfisher family, native to Africa and Asia, with an unusual self-defence tactic. It turns around and sprays the would-be attacker in the eyes with a torrent of thick, gooey diarrhoea. Then, for good measure, the hoopoe bathes in its own poop and bottom-slime to make itself wholly un-delicious.

4 Stink Spray – **Skunks** are famously stinky animals. But until you've been sprayed by one, you have no idea how stinky. When alarmed, skunks stamp their front feet and hiss. If that doesn't work, they stand on their hands, lift their tails and squirt a foul-smelling musk all over you. The musk travels up to 4 metres, and skunks have incredible aim. The musk smell is suffocatingly bad, and if it gets in your eyes it can cause temporary blindness.

5 **Blood Spray** – **Horned lizards** live in the deserts of North America and have the freakish and revolting habit of *squirting blood from their eyes*. They do this by squeezing their sinus cavities, bursting blood vessels and forcing a jet of blood from the corner of each eye. The blood contains a foul-smelling chemical that deters predators. Just in case, you know, the *sight* of this isn't off-putting enough . . .

6 **Bum Syrup** – When attacked by sharks or dolphins, **sperm whales** dump massive clouds of **anal syrup** (basically poo mixed with an oily goo squeezed from glands inside the bum) into the water, creating a foul stinky smoke-screen to cover their escape. They can do this up to *eight times in a row* if necessary.

7 **Snot Bubble** – **Hagfish** are, perhaps, the most horrid creatures on the planet. They look like a thick, headless, swimming tentacle. They burrow into the rotting bodies of dead animals and eat their way out. And worst of all, they surround themselves with thick, snotty, fish-stinking mucus – a slime layer so foul that any fish foolish enough to eat it will foam at the gills and suffocate. Bleurgh.

8 **Bum Licking** – **Koalas** – those fluffy, adorable, marsupial teddy-bears of Australia – might not seem quite so cute, once you hear what they get up to. Like all young mammals, koala babies drink their mother's milk. But at seven months of age, just before shifting to a diet of tough eucalyptus leaves, they line their stomachs with bacteria from their mother's gut. How? By licking poo from her furry bottom. There – see. You'll never look at a koala the same way again.

9 **Drool Sucking** – When **houseflies** land on your sandwich, they 'taste' it with special receptors in their feet, then drool a juicy mixture of saliva and digestive enzymes on to your food. The enzymes help liquefy the food, so that the fly can suck it back up again. Given that they do the same thing when they land on dog poop, it's not a great idea to let flies land on your food.

10 **Toilet Dining** – **Three-toed sloths**, found in the jungles of Central and South America, have been known to clamber down from the trees by night, crawl into campsites and eat human poo from camp toilets. No one knows why on earth they would want do this.

Thanks to their preference for the gory and bloody, another class of animals we just can't seem to stomach are **scavengers**. In particular, **carrion feeders** and **necrophages**.

What does that mean?

In other words: **animals that eat dead things**.

On the face of it, this doesn't make much sense. After all, we *all* eat dead things.

Herbivores eat dead plants, **carnivores** eat dead animals, and **omnivores** (including dogs, chimps and humans) eat *both*.

As most people see it, eating cooked chicken flesh in a curry is fine. But eating a raw, dead pheasant at the roadside is not.

Particularly if it has been sitting there for a while . . .

So eating dead things, to humans, is not *automatically* repulsive. It all depends on **what kind of dead thing** it is, **how recently** it died, and (perhaps) whether somebody took the trouble to **roast**, **grill** or **barbecue** it.

What makes a scavenger?

Think of the word 'scavenger', and what's the first thing that springs to mind?

A scampering rat? A growling hyena? A squawking vulture?

All these animals are scavengers, of course. But in fact, *all* animals will become scavengers if they're hungry enough. And some do it simply because it's easy.

Rats are the ultimate urban scavengers. It has been said that in big cities like London, New York and Tokyo, you're never more than 3 metres from a rat. Rats search for food in cellars, dustbins, food cupboards, anywhere they can find it. They eat dead **birds** on our rooftops, dead **squirrels** from our roadsides and — if they're hungry enough — **each other** (rats drown in our sewers all the time, and as far as the other rats are concerned, it's 'waste not, want not').

Knowing this, it is understandable that we might see a rat and be a little grossed out. But other rodents are just as bad. Left to their own ends, hungry **mice**, **gerbils**, **hamsters** and **guinea pigs** will *all* become scavengers eventually. As will other pets like rabbits and chinchillas. So why are we grossed out by rats and not the others? After all, it's not *their* fault they don't get nice clean bedding and fresh food every day. (As a matter of fact, rats make better pets than hamsters, gerbils and guinea pigs. They're smarter, friendlier and more affectionate with their owners!)

What about hyenas – those grisly, laughing, corpse-chompers of the African plains?

Yes, they scavenge the kills of lions and leopards. And they will happily chomp through the bones of any dead bird, cat, deer, dog or human they can find.

But are these wild dogs so different from the pampered pooches we keep in our homes? In a word, no.

Wild canines like **hyenas**, **dingoes**, **wolves**, **coyotes** and **jackals** make a living out of scavenging dead things – eating at least as many 'found' things as 'hunted'. But left to run wild, domestic dogs will do the same. Not just the wild-looking **Dobermanns** and **pit bulls** either. **Poodles**, **collies**, **corgis**, **whippets**, **dachshunds** and **Labradors** will all munch away on dead things, given an empty belly and few other options. A dog might be man's best friend while he's alive. But ask any veteran ambulance driver, and you'll get the full story. Many a pet terrier has been found chewing guiltily on the leg of its recently deceased owner rather than starve.

MUNCH!

Cats are no better. In Africa, proud, majestic **lions** scavenge almost as many cheetah kills as hyenas do. In the Americas, **pumas** and **jaguars** will happily take a day off hunting if there's a dead deer or armadillo lying around – even if it's several days old.

In the **Aves** (bird) family, handsome **bald eagles** will scavenge just like ugly **vultures** if they get hungry enough, and **kestrels** will eat from the same roadsides as **crows**.

Grizzly bears eat as much carrion as they do fresh fish, **giant pandas** eat bird and monkey remains along with bamboo, and **polar bears** will happily chew through week-old whales and walruses.

According to palaeontologists, even majestic dinosaurs like the terrifying *Tyrannosaurus rex* scavenged as much as they hunted. And so the list goes on.

Looked at this way, scavenging – or eating carrion – isn't so odd after all. So to be fair, we should be *every bit* as disgusted by lions and pandas as we are by hyenas and vultures.

*Some think T. rex scavenged **more** than it hunted. After all, it would have found it tricky to hold down wriggling prey with those stubby little arms . . .*

How about this: we could decide that *none* of these animals is revolting. After all, most don't *choose* to be scavengers. It's all about survival. Scavengers are just doing what they do, and we really have no right to *hate* them for it.

That makes sense. I guess...

Now I'm not saying you should go out and hug a hyena or anything. But then you shouldn't try to hug a panda or polar bear either...

Top 10 Corpse-Eating Animals

1 **Carrion Crow (*Corvus corone*)** – The world's most common roadkill-scoffing bird is also one of the world's cleverest. Eats grain, eggs, live insects, earthworms and mice. But also dead things of all kinds, wherever it can find them. Found throughout Europe and Asia.

2 **Lammergeier (*Gypaetus barbatus*)** – Large bearded vulture that lives in the mountains of southern Europe, central Asia, and Africa. Specializes in feeding on bones and bone marrow. Can swallow lamb bones whole (its name means 'lamb vulture' in German), and cracks the bones of larger animals by carrying them to up to 150 metres and dropping them on to rocky ground. Also known to do this to live tortoises.

3 **Marabou Stork (*Leptoptilos crumeniferus*)** – Huge ugly carcass-eating stork native to eastern and southern Africa. Stands over 1.5 metres tall, and has a wingspan of up to 3 metres. Shoves its bald, featherless head into corpses left half-eaten by lions.

4 **California Condor (*Gymnogyps californianus*)** – The world's largest raptor (bird of prey) lives in the western United States and, like the Marabou stork, measures 3 metres from wingtip to wingtip. They soar to heights of 4,500 metres and land to feast on dead cattle and deer. Condors almost went extinct in the 1970s and are still threatened with extinction today.

5 **Spotted Hyena** *(Crocuta crocuta)* - Fierce, intelligent dog-like scavenger of the African plains. Hyenas hunt in packs to bring down live zebra, gemsbok and wildebeest. But more often, they let lions, leopards and cheetahs do the killing, and simply mob them to steal their kills. Their powerful jaws can crush even the largest bones, and their tough stomachs can digest hair, hoofs and horns (any undigested bits are spewed up as 'bone pellets').

6 **Coyote** *(Canis latrans)* - Also known as the American Jackal or Brush Wolf. Probably the most adaptable canine on the planet. Found in the deserts, mountains, forests and (occasionally) cities of North America. Coyotes eat rabbits, rodents, fish (they are good swimmers), frogs, venomous snakes, pet cats and dogs . . . pretty much anything, dead or alive.

7 **Burying Beetle** *(Nicrophorus americanus)* - Small black-and-orange beetle native to North America. Belongs to a large family of carrion beetles (*Silphidaei*), which bury corpses and raise their young on them. Pairs of burying beetles may move a dead mouse or bird several metres to find soft soil suitable for grave-digging. After burial, the beetles strip the corpse of fur and feathers, lay eggs on the body and cover it with antibacterial slime to prevent it from rotting too quickly.

8 **Virginia Opossum** *(Didelphis virginiana)* - Hairy, rat-tailed, cat-sized mammals found throughout North and Central America. The only marsupials (pouch-bearing mammals) found outside Australia, opossums are nocturnal scavengers that eat insects, worms and dead things aplenty. When threatened by a predator, they 'play dead' by rolling on their backs and releasing a foul odour, which makes it smell as if they've been rotting for weeks.

9 **Tasmanian Devil** *(Sarcophilus harrisii)* - Stocky dog-like mammal found only on the southern Australian island of Tasmania, where they're often seen dining on roadkill by night. Like coyotes, devils will eat pretty much anything, but their favourite food is a fat dead wombat. Their scientific name, *Sarcophilus*, means 'likes dead things' in Latin.

10 **Komodo Dragon** *(Varanus komodoensis)* - The largest living member of the lizard *(Squamatai)* family, these living dragons grow up to 3 metres long, and weigh up to 160 kilograms. They are found only on the Indonesian islands of Komodo, Rintja, Padar and Flores, where they stalk live deer and water buffalo and sniff out corpses from several miles away.

Know Your Poop

Try this tricky, plop-themed crossword, and test your knowledge of the great number two . . .

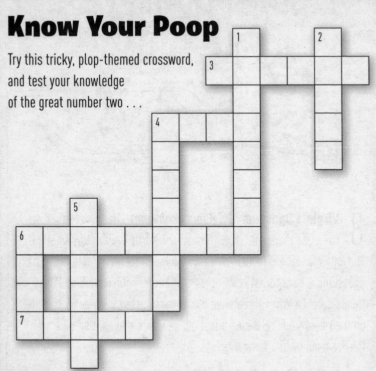

Across

3. Poo used as fertilizer; often from pigs or horses
4. Plop dropped by wild carnivores (e.g. bears)
6. Name given to little balls of poop dropped by small animals (e.g. gerbils, rabbits)
7. Bat or bird poo

Down

1. Worm droppings
2. The tiny poops of caterpillars and leaf-eating insects
4. Otter plops
5. Sloppy, disk-shaped poo dropped by cattle
6. Bulky poo type, favoured by beetles

Answers on page 154

BETTER OUT THAN IN

The Science of Icky, Sticky Body Fluids

Mine are fine, Yours are yuck!

SNIFF! SNIFF!

Would You Rather...

- Have a hard poo or a watery poo?
- Smell a fresh stool or have fresh drool on your skin?
- Be peed at or vomited at?

We don't have to go far to find things that disgust us. In fact, our own bodies — and the things that **drip**, **ooze** and **spray** out of them — are a common cause of **revulsion** the world over.

The sight and smell of bodily fluids, like **blood, sweat** and **saliva**, can make us feel so ill that we want to **vomit**. Oddly, we are often fine with our own fluids. But not those belonging to others.

In other words, *my* blood, sweat and spit are okay, but *yours* are disgusting. The same goes for **snot**, **sweat** and **phlegm**. And while few of us enjoy seeing or smelling our own poo, seeing or smelling *someone else's* poo is just **gross**.

So why should that be? Why are natural body wastes so revolting to us? And why yours, more than mine?

What's in a number two?

Let's start with the biggest, most obvious substance to regularly exit the human body — faeces. Otherwise known as excrement, jobbies, brown trout, number twos or simply **poo**.

Why is poo so disgusting?

I mean, seriously — we make the stuff. It comes out of our own bodies. So why should it be so **repulsive** to us? Babies don't seem to mind having poo on them. And as we've learned, some animals eat, sleep and live in their own poo. So what's our problem with poo?

To understand that, we first have to look at what poo is made of. The average human adult drops about **100–250 grams** of poo per day. Kids a little less. About 75 per cent of every healthy 'bog log' is water. (More if you have diarrhoea — but we'll come to that later on.) The remaining 25 per cent is chunky solid matter.

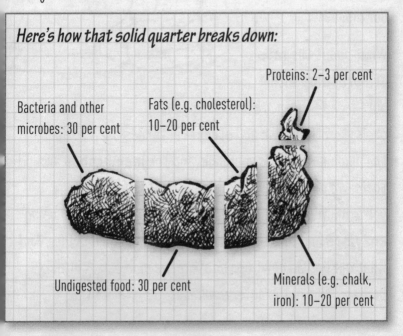

Here's how that solid quarter breaks down:

Proteins: 2–3 per cent

Bacteria and other microbes: 30 per cent

Fats (e.g. cholesterol): 10–20 per cent

Undigested food: 30 per cent

Minerals (e.g. chalk, iron): 10–20 per cent

Now take a look at this list of ingredients, and see if you can figure out which one turns us off.

Mashed-up, **undigested food** is pretty gross, I guess. But most of the foody stuff you find in poo is simply **cellulose** – a plant fibre humans cannot digest. Cellulose is used to build plant cell walls, and it's what makes celery and lettuce so crunchy. Cows and other herbivores can digest it, but humans cannot. So it passes through our digestive systems and helps give **solid structure** to our poos. Not so hideous to think about, is it? Surely, this can't be the source of our disgust.

BLAH!

What about the **fats** and **proteins** within our faeces? These are solid lumps of cholesterol, bilirubin and other substances used to build the machinery inside your cells and the **membranes** around them. We eat fats and proteins in the form of milk, egg yolks, marbled meat and bacon rinds. We digest them using **enzymes** and **bile salts** from the liver and gallbladder. And what our bodies can't use or store, we plop out. A bit icky, perhaps. But not exactly *revolting*.

Likewise, there's nothing particularly *horrible* about inorganic **minerals**, such as **calcium carbonate** (chalk), **calcium phosphate**, and **iron oxide**. Some of these we get from our food. Since we only need tiny amounts of most minerals to stay healthy, our bodies simply let the rest drop out. The iron oxide comes from the breakdown of red blood cells. When these cells reach the end of their lives, they are broken up by the liver, releasing an iron-rich protein called **bilirubin**. As gut bacteria feed on this, they oxidize (i.e. rust) the iron within it, turning it rusty brown. This is largely what gives your poo its healthy brown hue. Rust in your poo might seem a little strange. But again, it's not exactly *repulsive*. Next!

The final ingredient in poo — and the one that usually makes up most of its solid mass — is **bacteria**. All 1.5 metres of the large intestine are coated with a thick lining of bacteria. The average human gut contains up to **100 trillion bacterial cells**, of over 1,000 different species.

BACTERIA

SMALL INTESTINE

LARGE INTESTINE

STOMACH

BACTERIA

Most are harmless, or even helpful – mopping up nutrients we cannot digest for ourselves, or taking up space in the intestine so that nasty, harmful bacteria cannot set up shop in there. It is these 'possibly harmful' bacteria that are at the root of our disgust with poo.

That makes sense . . . I guess. How harmful can these 'bad' bacteria be?

About 500 of the microbe species commonly found in poo can cause disease when they're ingested (accidentally eaten or transferred to the mouth). These include bacteria such as *Eschericia coli* (*E. coli*) and *Vibrio cholerae*, along with protozoa like *Giardia* and *Entamoeba*. When these organisms infect your gut, grow out of control or produce toxic chemicals as they feed, they cause diseases like **cholera**, **typhoid**, **salmonella** and **giardiasis**.

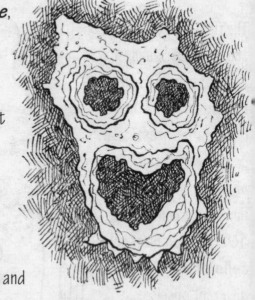

This *Entamoeba* bacteria looks like a scary clown and can kill you in days.

These nasty diseases cause severe **diarrhoea** and **dehydration**, and can prove deadly in places where **antibiotics** are not available.

This is why we are so disgusted by poo (and in particular *other people's* poo). Through experience, we have learned that getting other people's poo on us is a great way to develop a nasty **gut disease**. So over time, the very thought of poo on our skin — or worse yet, our *tongues* — makes us screw up our faces and recoil in disgust.

Just another **safety tactic** our brains have evolved, to keep us **safe from harm**.

Top 10 Reasons for a Colourful Poo

We all know that poo is brown. Only sometimes, it isn't!
So what does it mean when your **poo changes hue**?

Poo colour has been used to **predict disease** in traditional Chinese medicine for thousands of years, and is still used by doctors today. But it might just be a sign that you're eating too many **sweets and cakes** . . .

1 **Brown** – Chestnut or chocolate brown is, of course, the typical colour for freshly-dropped human faeces. The brown colour comes from a chemical called **bilirubin**, which is made when **old red blood cells** are broken down in the liver and passed to the gut for excretion.

2 **Grey** – when your poo goes a **stony grey**, it means little or no bilirubin is present. This can be a **sign of liver disease** (hepatitis), which prevents the proper breakdown of old blood cells.

3 **White** – very pale poo is often caused by **gallstones** – painful crystalline pebbles that develop inside the **gallbladder**. Once formed, these tiny stones may slip into the bile duct, blocking the flow of bilirubin from the liver to the gut and robbing your poo of its hue.

4 **Yellow** – buttercup-coloured poo can also be a sign of **liver problems**. But it might be a sign that your bowels are infected with a **gut-dwelling parasite** called *giardia*.

We'll learn more about giardia, and other parasitic creatures, in the next chapter. Wheeee!

5 **Orange** – having a tangerine-coloured poo is rare. But it can happen to **vegetarians** or **vegans** who eat loads of **carrots**, **sweet potatoes**, **apricots** or **pumpkins**. You really do have to eat a *lot* of orange-coloured stuff to make this happen, though. More likely, your jaffa poo was the result of

eating cakes or sweets with **artificial food colouring.**

6 **Red** – blood-red faeces are a real danger sign, as they are usually caused by **bleeding in the colon** (large intestine), close to the rectum (the – ahem – exit). Most often, bloody poos are caused by swollen blood vessels in or around the rectum, called **haemorrhoids**, or **piles**. That said, you can also get a red/purple poo from eating too much beetroot, tomato juice or food colouring . . .

7 **Green** – leafy-green logs can be a sign of **gastroenteritis** – an infection of the stomach or small intestine. They may also be caused by eating very large quantities of green veggies, or by **rapid bowel transit** – high-speed pooing brought on by drinking strong coffee or tea.

8 **Blue** – outside of butterflies and birds, the colour blue is **rare in nature**, and human bodies are no exception. So if you drop a bright blue poo, the colour is all **artificial**. That means you almost certainly ate too much birthday cake yesterday.

9 **Black** – very dark or jet-black plops can be a **bad sign** indeed. Often they contain dark **clotted blood** from the stomach or small intestine. But you can also get them from eating lots of liquorice and blueberries.

10 **Multi-coloured** – contrary to popular belief, clowns and unicorns do not have rainbow-coloured poo. Neither do sick people. So if you **poop a rainbow**, it means only one thing: it's time to cut down on the Skittles!

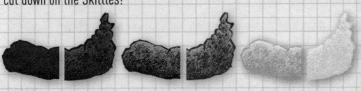

Too dark   Healthy   Too light

Tummy Trouble

Healthy poo is gross enough. Unhealthy poo can get *really* disgusting.

Diarrhoea is the name given to **loose, watery poo** that exits the body much faster than usual. It can last anywhere from half an hour to **several days**. It can be a sign of **food poisoning** or **food allergies** that cause swelling in the intestines. But more often it is a sign of an **infection** somewhere in the gut. A wide range of **bacteria** and **viruses** can infect the gut and cause diarrhoeal diseases, and worldwide there are over 1.7 billion cases of runny-poo disease every year.

Most cases clear up on their own, as your **immune system** fights off the infection. But serious infections can cause acute diarrhoeal diseases leading to **dehydration** (water loss) and **malnutrition** (nutrient loss). Left untreated — as it is often is in developing countries — this can be *deadly*.

So what happens during diarrhoea? Why do gut infections make your poo runny, rather than, say, just a funny colour?

Basically, it comes down to this – the intestines have different jobs, and when the large intestine can't do its job, you're in trouble.

The **small intestine** is divided into **three parts** – the **duodenum**, the **jejunum** and the **ileum**. In an adult human it can grow up to **10 metres** long, but measures only 3 centimetres in diameter. Its main job is to **digest** and **absorb proteins**, **fats** and **sugars** from your food – already broken up and liquefied by your **teeth**, your **saliva**, your **stomach acids** and **bile** (more on that in a minute).

The **large intestine** (or colon) encircles the bundled-up small intestine. It is roughly 1.5 metres long, and 6 centimetres in diameter – more than **twice as wide** as the small intestine. The large intestine mops up any nutrients not absorbed by its little brother, the small intestine. But its main job is to **absorb water**.

*This is where it gets its name. Your small intestine is much **longer**, but your large intestine is far **fatter**.*

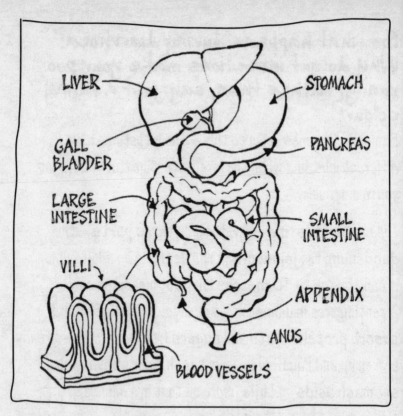

LIVER

STOMACH

GALL BLADDER

PANCREAS

LARGE INTESTINE

SMALL INTESTINE

VILLI

APPENDIX

ANUS

BLOOD VESSELS

Sloppy, watery **chyme** exits the small intestine, and becomes dried out and is compacted into solid **faeces** (poo) in the colon. The chyme contains a mixture of **water**, **undigested food** and **enzymes** from the liver. Inside the large intestine, this flows past thousands of tiny fleshy bumps called **villi**, which line the inside of the intestine.

When it all works well, the villi pull **water**, **enzymes** and **nutrients** out of the contents of the colon and leave solid (but slippery) faeces behind.

But when the gut is infected by **harmful bacteria** or **viruses**, the lining of the large intestine swells, and the villi cannot **absorb** much water from the chyme. The result is **water-logged poo**, which — depending on how severe the problem is — trickles, drops or *explodes* from your bottom.

To make matters worse, the muscle that ordinarily holds your bottom shut (the **anal sphincter**) can sense the pressure of solid faeces — allowing you to *decide* when to poo, once the urge arises. But it cannot sense the difference between gas (i.e. farts) and liquid poos (i.e. diarrhoea). So what feels like a harmless bottom-burp can turn into something *far, far worse* ...

With a nasty bout of **diarrhoea**, you might squirt up to **20 litres** (42 pints!) of gooey poo from your bottom in a single day. Along with the water, you lose all the **nutrients**, **minerals** and **vitamins** your body failed to digest.

NOT AGAIN!

It's easy to see how, if this goes on for days and days, this could make you very weak and feeble indeed. So if you *do* get diarrhoea, be sure to **drink lots of water** – ideally with a little **sugar** and **salt** dissolved in it – to help replace all that you lose. And stay close to the toilet . . .

Top 10 Names for Diarrhoea Around the Globe

The word diarrhoea comes from a Greek phrase meaning 'flowing through'. Here's what others prefer to call it . . .

Runs, Trots, Bum Slurry (UK)

Butt Soup, Hershey Squirts, Green-Apple Splatters (USA)

Scutters, Dingbats (Australia)

Skitters (Canada)

Durchfall (Germany)

Fuxie (China)

Kuhara (Africa)

Geri (Japan)

Ponos (Russia)

Chorro (South America)

In German, durch = 'through' and 'geri' is written with two Japanese kanji characters, which together say 'lower illness'.

94

Disgusting Digestion

So poo (solid, explosive or otherwise) repels us because it signals disease. Does the same go for other body fluids too?

Like poo, **saliva**, **vomit** and **urine** are all natural parts of the human **digestive system**. But nobody wants anybody else's spit, puke or pee on them, if they can help it. And most of us are absolutely *disgusted* by the idea of *swallowing* them. Here's why . . .

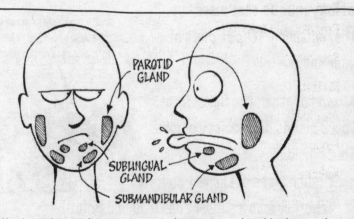

PAROTID GLAND

SUBLINGUAL GLAND

SUBMANDIBULAR GLAND

Saliva is a mixture of water, mucus and enzymes produced in the mouth by your **salivary glands**. There are **three pairs** of salivary glands in your mouth, which work together to make saliva. These are the **parotid glands**, the **submandibular glands** and the **sublingual glands**.

The **parotid glands** are large glands that lie close to your jaw hinges, just in front of your ears. They are connected to the roof of your mouth by two tubes, called parotid ducts. The parotid glands produce a **pale, watery fluid** that makes up about **20 per cent** of the total volume of saliva in your mouth.

The **submandibular glands** sit in the lower jaw or mandible (*submandibular* means 'under the jaw' in Latin). They squirt out a **pale yellow, protein-rich fluid** that makes up about **70 per cent** of your saliva.

The **sublingual glands** sit beneath the tongue (in Latin, sub means 'under', *lingua* means 'tongue') and squirt out a **thick, sticky mucus** that makes up the remaining **10 per cent** of your saliva.

In case you hadn't figured it out, that's also where the English word language *comes from.*

Mixed together, the fluids from these glands do a variety of jobs. These include:

- binding globs of chewed-up food together into a slippery ball (called a **bolus**) which slide easily down the throat without getting stuck
- **lubricating** (greasing up) your throat, making it easier to swallow

- **dissolving** sugars, acids and proteins, allowing your taste buds to absorb and detect flavours
- breaking down starches, using an enzyme called **amylase**
- washing the whole mouth, removing food debris and keeping the mouth (relatively) clean.

Of course, saliva doesn't completely succeed in this last task. It *tries* to keep your mouth clean and tidy, but it really can't keep up.

So our mouths are 'dirty' then?

Like your intestines, your mouth is a haven for **billions** of bacteria. Even if you brush your teeth and rinse with mouthwash daily, you still have up to **500 species** of bacteria living in your mouth, and about **100,000 bacteria** living *on every tooth*. If you don't brush your teeth, you might have 1,000 species living in there, and a billion bacteria per tooth!

Stinky mouth bacteria are also the cause of morning 'dragon breath'. Since the flow of saliva slows or stops during sleep, bacteria are free to feed, grow and party all night long. In some cases, this can develop into **halitosis** – the medical name for *really* bad breath. Breath that smells like sour milk and rotten eggs.

Now here's the thing – most of the bacteria that live in our mouths are completely harmless. But certain viruses – including **measles**, **chickenpox**, **influenza** (flu) and cold viruses – are passed from person to person through **snot**, **spit** and **mucus** that end up in the mouth. So while we are sometimes happy to swap spit with people we *really* like (during kissing), having a stranger (especially one who *looks* ill) spit or drool on us disgusts us, as it is connected to sickness and disease.

What about puke? When I see puke, I want to puke!

Vomit and **bile**, while icky to see and smell, serve natural functions in the body too. Vomiting clears the stomach of rotten or **toxic** food, helping us to avoid **lethal poisoning** when we eat 'off' foods, scoff poisonous mushrooms or drink too much alcohol. (Rats, interestingly, cannot vomit. Which makes them very vulnerable to rat poison.)

*Vomiting **helps** with this, but doesn't always **succeed**. Which is why you can still die from food and alcohol poisoning. So don't go eating poisonous mushrooms, thinking that your vomit will save you. It may not...*

If you vomit enough, and your entire stomach is emptied, then you might begin to see **bile** as you continue to retch and spew. Bile is a **bitter-tasting**, **yellow-green fluid** which contains a wide range of **salts** and **enzymes** – both of which help to digest fats in your food. Bile is made in the liver, stored and concentrated in the **gallbladder**, then passed to the small intestine through the **bile duct**. If you vomit enough, bile can be squeezed up into your empty stomach, and ejected from the mouth.

As with saliva, vomit and bile are not particularly dangerous fluids. But vomiting food and bile is not just a sign of poisoning. It is also a common side effect of **infection** and **disease**. **Influenza**, **norovirus**, **meningitis** and **gastroenteritis** can all cause vomiting. And though we are unlikely to swallow anyone's vomit or bile, the *presence* of it is enough to disgust us, as it warns us that 'there lies disease'!

So once again, our disgust is a signal to ourselves (and perhaps to others) that we should all stay away from something. Spit, vomit and bile are icky because we recognize them as *unsafe*.

One possible exception to this 'icky = unsafe' rule is **urine**. Most of us find the idea of being peed on, or drinking urine, pretty disgusting.

Yet actually, urine is more or less **sterile**. Filtered and produced in the **kidneys**, it contains very few bacteria. And hardly any bacterial or viral diseases are passed from person to person via urine.

So why are we disgusted by it then?

It could just be that we think of urine in the same category as snot, poo, vomit and other 'disgusting waste fluids'. Who knows? Some people aren't bothered by urine at all. Some even *drink it on purpose* (ugh), claiming that it helps keep your **digestive system** healthy.

In any case — given the strange, horrid choice — most people would *much* rather be peed on than vomited on, or pooped on. So maybe pee isn't quite so disgusting after all . . .

BOTTOMS UP!

Icky Science
Expert 3

I study how poop works.

Dr William Parker, Duke University

What's your job title and what do you study?

Officially I'm an Associate Professor in the Duke Medical Science Research Department. My work takes me in all kinds of unexpected directions, and my team studies lots of things. I study the worms and bacteria that live inside our guts, how diseases develop, what the appendix is for, and much, much more. Right now, we're looking at how poop works.

Why? How does that benefit the world?

It offers new approaches to treating all kinds of diseases. Medicine likes to start with a disease and try to figure out what causes it. But one of the problems with that approach is that you might not know what 'normal' is. And you really need to understand 'normal' before you can fully understand a disease process. So we've been trying to find out what 'normal' poop is – what it looks like, what it contains, how it works and so on.

To do this, we take poop samples and tissue samples from people with specific diseases, and compare them with samples from healthy people. All poop contains bacteria. But what we've discovered is that 'healthy poop' and 'diseased poop' contain different types of bacteria and worms. And it turns out that some kinds of bacteria (and *even* worms) are very important for good health (a bit like the 'good bacteria' you hear about in yogurt adverts).

What else have you discovered?

Along the way, we also discovered that the human appendix – once thought useless in the human body – is actually a kind of storehouse for these 'good' bacteria. During illness, we often lose our 'good' bacteria to bouts of diarrhoea. Afterwards, your gut could easily become a home for nasty bacteria which cause disease. So the appendix is there to supply reinforcements, which settle the intestines and crowd out the 'bad guys' before they can move in.

We've also learned that some autoimmune diseases – like asthma, migraines and coeliac disease – hardly ever occur in the developing world, where most people have some kind of benign (harmless) flatworm living in their gut. So it may well be that we all need a worm to stay healthy! Maybe one day we'll be treating certain diseases by giving patients a worm, rather than a pill or vaccine.

What first got you interested in science?

A really great teacher, who taught science at my school. He would ignore the tests and textbooks, do experiments just for the fun of it and encourage us to come up with our own ideas for class experiments and science projects.

What's the most disgusting thing you've ever seen or done in connection with your job?

We had this big freezer in the lab with all kinds of frozen samples in it. Poop samples, breast milk, bits of human organs . . . you name it. Then one summer we had a power cut and the freezer broke. Only nobody noticed, because the lab was empty all that month.

By the time we finally came back and opened it, everything inside had turned into a single huge slimy mass. And the smell . . . I just cannot describe it.

I've been sprayed by a skunk before, and that doesn't even come close to how bad this smell was. (Shudder.) Sometimes I still smell it in my sleep . . .

Blood, Pus and Scabs

Would You Rather...

- See blood ooze from a gash or squirt from a severed artery?
- Smell a pus-filled wound or pop a blood-filled blister?
- Pick someone's scabs or pop their zits?

So what else is considered gross when it squirts or oozes from the body?

Fresh blood from a fresh wound? Thick, **yellowish pus** from an old one?

Mmmmm, nice. (Not.)

Blood is actually a fascinating substance. It is the main transport system of the human body.

It gets its colour from **erythrocytes** (red blood cells), which transport **oxygen** from the **lungs** to tissues and **organs** throughout the body, and carry **toxic carbon dioxide** back to the lungs to be breathed out.

It also contains **leucocytes** (white blood cells), the **self-defence force** of the human body. These tiny guardians

105

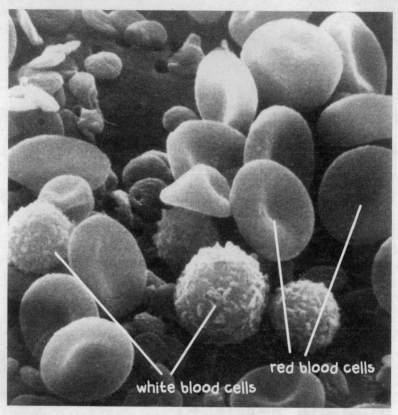

red blood cells

white blood cells

locate, target and attack harmful invaders — including bacteria and **protists** (single-celled parasites like amoebas). Some white blood cells even destroy cells infected by viruses, to stop them from multiplying and spreading. And it is white blood cells (specifically, **B lymphocytes**) that produce **antibodies** — making us immune to diseases we have already encountered.

We'll learn more about antibodies and immunity in the next chapter.

Blood carries lots of other things too, including:

- **platelets** – simple proteins that clot together to plug wounds after an injury
- **hormones** – complex proteins that carry signals between the brain and other organs
- **lipoproteins** – carrier proteins that bind and transport fats (like cholesterol)
- **sugars**, **salts**, **minerals**, **amino acids** – essential nutrients needed to build and power your cells and tissues.

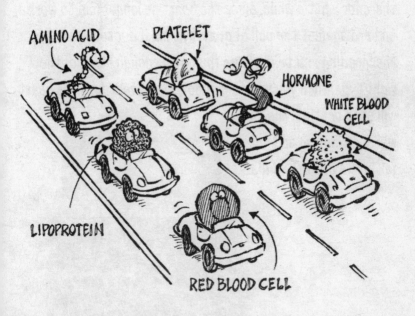

Without a constant supply of oxygen, sugars and salts, your **brain** and **nervous system** would shut down within minutes. Only your blood can carry these things. So if your

blood stops moving (say, after a **heart attack**), your brain cannot get the things it needs and you fall **unconscious**. If you're lucky, doctors will be able to restart your heart and get the blood moving again. If not, you will fall into a coma and die.

Likewise, if you lose too much blood – from a deep **cut** or **puncture wound** – your **blood pressure** drops, and your heart cannot pump hard enough to get it to the brain.

Falling down (**fainting**) will help get the remaining blood up there for a little while, since the heart no longer has to work so hard against the pull of **gravity**. And if doctors can stop the bleeding and **transfuse** (pump in) enough blood of the right type, then you'll be fine. If not, then eventually the heart will stop beating, the blood will stop moving and you'll fall into a **coma** and die.

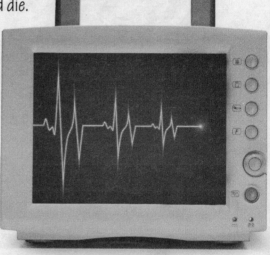

That explains why losing blood is scary. But does that really explain why seeing someone lose blood is gross?

In a way, yes. As we've already seen with **edible spiders** and **explosive poo**, fear and disgust are closely connected. Often we think we're disgusted by something, when we are actually just afraid of it.

If you **faint** at the sight of blood, it is because you are so afraid of the *idea* of losing blood that your brain triggers an emergency response that doctors call **shock**. This closes off blood vessels in your arms, legs and belly, which prevents rapid blood loss from wounded limbs *and* diverts precious blood away from the **digestive system**. This is why your hands go cold and clammy, your knees go weak and your stomach feels queasy right before you faint.

SWOOON!

LOOK!

Over time, some people begin to confuse this 'weak and queasy' sensation with the feeling of **revulsion** or **disgust**. So while they think they are disgusted by blood and gore, they are actually just afraid of it. The good news is, this fear (and disgust)

For more about this, see **Stuff That Scares Your Pants Off!**, a book all about fears and phobias.

NOTHING TO WORRY ABOUT!

can be overcome, as any surgeon or vet will tell you.

That said, fresh, gushing blood is one thing. **Blood** and **pus** oozing from scabs and sores is quite another ...

What is pus then? Where does it come from?

Pus is mostly made up of **white blood cells** that flock to the site of an injury to combat infections. Wherever the skin is broken, there is the danger that **harmful bacteria** might get in through the break, set up shop in the wound and get into the nearby tissues and the **bloodstream**. So our bodies respond by forming **clots** (triggered by **platelets** close to

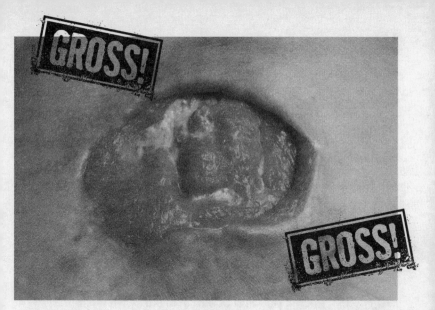

the site of the wound) to plug cracks and holes in the skin, and by sending **leucocytes** (white blood cells) to fight off any bacteria that might already have made it through.

The result is a wound filled with oozing, yellow-white pus. The worse the infection by bacteria, the bigger the battle, and the more pus there is. If all goes well, then the bugs are fought off, the wound closes over and a **scab** is formed over the site until fresh skin (or **fibrous scar tissue**) can grow and permanently close the gap.

If not, then pus may continue to ooze from the wound for days, as the **leucocytes** fight a losing battle and the **infection spreads** to other areas.

How delightful.

Some infectious diseases, such as **scabies**, **impetigo** and **bubonic plague**, also cause pus-filled scabs and blisters to form on the skin. In ancient and medieval times, people would often die of **infected wounds**, and from **infectious diseases** that spread through contact with open sores and scabs. But ever since we started using **antiseptics** – and more recently bacteria-battling **antibiotics** – deaths from infections like these have become rare.

In any case, oozing pus and scabs still carry with them a fear of infection and disease. So for the most part, we are disgusted by them because of our fear of disease – even when the condition (as with **eczema**, **psoriasis** and **acne**) is not contagious, so you can't 'catch' anything anyway.

OH GOODIE!

And for the gross-out fans among you, don't worry – we'll learn about some *genuinely* disgusting diseases in the next chapter . . .

Last on the list of revolting body wastes are **snot**, **phlegm** and **sweat**.

As with the other body fluids, the rule seems to be 'if it's *mine*, it's fine'. But as for someone else's . . . well, let's just say we're not exactly thrilled at the thought of having *any* of these things **wiped** on us, **dribbled** on us, or (ackkkkk!) **fed** to us.

What's the difference between snot and phlegm?

They are both types of **mucus** that protect your respiratory system. The main difference between them (other than that snot is a bit more watery) is that **snot** is produced in the nose, while **phlegm** is produced in the airways (the **trachea** and **bronchi**) between your throat and lungs.

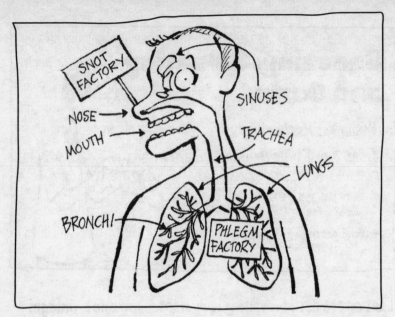

Their job is to trap dust, grime, bacteria, plant pollen, **fungal spores** and viruses trying to make their way up your nose, down your throat and into your lungs. The sticky mucus surrounds these invading nasties, which are then wafted toward the nose and mouth by tiny, moving hairs called **cilia**. Once in the nose or mouth, the snot and phlegm can be blown out, spat out or (ugh) swallowed.

Smokers often burn off the cilia lining their airways, leaving them unable to clear the phlegm. This is what gives many smokers that wet, rattling 'smoker's cough' – a sign that their lungs are in poor health, and could be vulnerable to infections and diseases such as bronchitis.

Yuck!

Gross as it seems, this keeps your airways and lungs clear, so that you can breathe properly. When

disease-causing nasties get deep into your lungs, they cause **infections** and **inflammation**, and *lots* of mucus is made to try to clear the problem.

Each **virus** or **bacterium** affects the system in a slightly different way. **Rhinoviruses** and **adenoviruses** cause colds, bringing with them a seemingly *endless* supply of fresh snot. Nasty colds can go on for weeks, your nose dribbling *litres* of the stuff each day. If it irritates the airways, snot may also be sneezed out of them at high speed, spraying **virus-laden snot droplets** several feet through the air.

Similarly, **influenza**, **bronchitis** and other types of bronchial (chest) infection can leave you coughing up phlegm until your throat is red raw.

Since snot and phlegm are basically *loaded* with nasty bacteria and viruses — and many diseases are spread between people via **airborne snot particles** — it is perhaps not surprising that we've learned to shy away from snotty, sneezing people with hacking coughs.

COUGH !!
SPLUTTER !!

As with blood, poo and vomit, it's the connection to disease that makes *other people's* snot and phlegm particularly revolting to us. As for our own — well, if you're sick *already*, you might as well snort that snot back up your nose, or swallow that phlegm you just coughed up, right?

Finally, we come to sticky, stinky **perspiration**. Otherwise known as sweat. This handy substance is produced by **sweat glands** in your skin, which come in one of two types.

Eccrine sweat glands are found pretty much all over the body, and are mostly there to help cool the body. When your

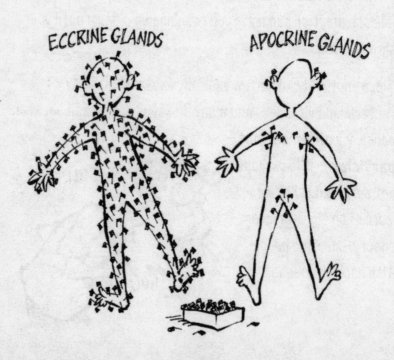

ECCRINE GLANDS

APOCRINE GLANDS

body temperature gets too high, your brain sends a signal to these glands, telling them to squeeze out some sweat — which is mostly water and **sodium chloride** (salt) taken from the bloodstream. As this salty liquid pools and evaporates off your body, it cools your skin and lowers your body temperature, cooling you down.

Apocrine sweat glands are found only in the ears and armpits and around the nipples and groin. They produce a slightly **thicker, sweeter type of sweat** loaded with body wastes and **pheromones**. These smelly chemical messengers (believe it or not) make us smell pleasant to members of the opposite sex.

I'm not convinced by this. My brother STINKS! That cannot be attractive to the opposite sex.

It's true. It's only when you don't wash the sweat off for a while that things start to go awry.

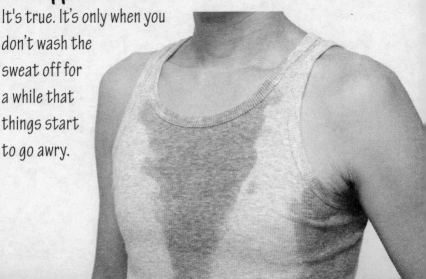

When sweat is left to pool and dry, bacteria living on the skin begin to feed on it, releasing nasty, foul-smelling waste products. Left long enough, these smells alone are enough to trigger our disgust at sweaty people. But to make things worse, many diseases also lead to **fever sweating**, which means we also tend to connect excessive (or particularly stinky) sweating with sickness and disease.

More about that in the next chapter...

Once again, it's fear that leads to disgust, whether it's called for or not.

Spare a thought, if you will, for sufferers of these sweating disorders. Some are common, others very rare. But it can't be much fun to have *any* of them . . .

Top 10 Strange Sweating Disorders

1 **Slippery Hands** (*palmar hyperhidrosis*) — Hyperhidrosis, or oversweating, is the most common form of sweat disorder. When it happens all over the body, it is called generalized hyperhidrosis, and is usually the sign of an underlying disease, such as **diabetes**. But rarer genetic diseases can cause eccrine sweat glands to overproduce sweat in some areas of the body only. Palmar hyperhidrosis gives you cold, wet, sweaty palms, sometimes all day long, sometimes triggered by **nervousness** or **anxiety**.

2 **Slippery Feet** (*plantar hyperhidrosis*) — Overactive sweat glands in the soles of the feet cause plantar hyperhidrosis, resulting in cold, slippery feet. Treacherous on tiled kitchen floors.

3 **Armpit Flooding** (*axillary hyperhidrosis*) — Overactive eccrine or apocrine glands in the armpits can cause a whole host of disorders. The simplest is boundless armpit sweat, which soaks through shirts and suits even on cold days, much to the sufferer's embarrassment.

4 **Food Sweats** (*gustatory hyperhidrosis*) — A form of oversweating that is triggered every time you eat or drink. Most of us sweat in this way when we eat particularly spicy food, which fools our bodies into thinking we are too hot. But for **gustatory hyperhidrosis** sufferers, it happens even when they eat ice cream.

5 **Sweat Hives** *(cholinergic urticaria)* – Cholinergic urticaria sufferers are, quite literally, **allergic** to their own sweat. On warm days, their sweat causes itchy, blotchy rashes that spread right across their bodies. A nightmare disease for sun-loving beach bunnies.

6 **Stinky Sweat** *(bromhidrosis)* – Anyone who fails to wash for a few days will be familiar with BO (body odour). But sufferers of **bromhidrosis** have particularly thick, sweet or nutritious sweat, causing faster bacterial growth and unpleasant odours within hours, rather than days.

7 **Coloured Sweat** *(chromhidrosis)* – A rare disorder of apocrine glands found in the face, armpits and nipples, which results in **brightly coloured sweat**. Sweat shades include yellow, green, blue, pink, milky white and jet black.

8 **Sweating Blood** *(haematidrosis)* – A rare disorder resulting from excess iron intake or certain liver diseases, resulting in blood oozing through your sweat glands instead of sweat. Also occasionally appears in otherwise healthy people facing extreme stress or danger.

9 **No Sweat** *(anhidrosis)* –Malfunctioning eccrine and apocrine glands cause this rare and dangerous disorder, which leaves you completely **unable to sweat**. Sufferers can quickly overheat on warm days, suffering brain damage or even **death**.

10 **Fish Odour Syndrome** *(trimethylaminuria)* –A rare **metabolic** disorder causes this unfortunate condition, in which the fish-smelling chemical **trimethylamine** is absorbed from food but cannot be broken down inside the body. Instead, it leaks from sweat glands and skin pores, making the sufferer smell like rotting fish. Nasty.

BUGS, PLAGUES AND PARASITES

The Science of Disgusting Diseases

Would You Rather . . .

- Have measles or migraines?
- Have a dangerous bug in your guts or a flesh-eating bug on your skin?
- Catch rabies or bubonic plague?

From **measles** and **chickenpox** to **migraines** and **meningitis**, *nobody* likes to be ill. Yet at some point in our lives, it's pretty much guaranteed that *all* of us will suffer from some type of illness or disease.

But what is disease, exactly? I mean, where do diseases come from?

Some diseases are passed around and caught. Others just seem to spring up all by themselves.

So what gives?

In medical terms, a **disease** is something that **prevents healthy living**. In other words, anything that **interferes** with the **essential functions of life**.

For humans and most other animals, these 'life functions' include:

- **respiration** (breathing)
- **circulation** (blood flow)
- **digestion** (feeding, or obtaining energy)
- **excretion** (getting rid of wastes)
- **growth** (getting bigger, and replacing old cells with new ones)
- **locomotion** (moving around)
- **sensitivity** (ability to think and sense the world around you)
- **reproduction** (making babies).

Diseases, then, are things that mess with these processes — **altering** or **stopping** them in ways that prevent your body from performing at its best.

Most diseases are recognized by their visible signs or **symptoms**. In other words, **symptoms** describe *how* a disease messes with your life.

To give a few examples . . .

Function	Disease	Symptom
respiration	colds, flu	breathing problems
circulation	Ebola	bleeding from skin and eyes
digestion	salmonella	vomiting
excretion	cholera	diarrhoea
growth	cancer	cells grow out of control
locomotion	muscular dystrophy	inability to move
sensitivity	cataracts	blurry vision or blindness
reproduction	infertility	cannot get pregnant

Using this list, we can figure out a few more things about diseases too.

First, some diseases mess with your life functions just **a little**, others **a lot**.

A nasty **cold** will affect your breathing by filling your nose, throat and chest with mucus. But it won't stop your breathing altogether, and usually does little more than make you feel bad for a while. **Cholera**, on the other hand, wreaks so much havoc in your gut that you (literally) poo yourself to death.

That's horrible! What else?

Second, some diseases are **visible**, others far **less** so. **Cholera** and **Ebola** both have obvious (and horrible) effects on the sufferer's body. But most forms of **cancer** do not. They develop unseen, inside the body. Which makes them *scary*, but not *disgusting*.

Go on . . .

Third, some diseases people are **born** with, while others are **caught** from other people or animals. You can't 'catch' **cancer** or **cataracts**. But you can certainly catch **Ebola** and **flu**. We call these **infectious** (or **contagious**) diseases.

All contagious diseases are infectious, but not all infectious diseases are contagious. Here's why. Infectious diseases are spread by germs (usually bacteria or viruses) entering the body – from soil, tabletops or anywhere at all. For a disease to be contagious, the germs must be passed from person to person. So there you go.

Fourth, the diseases that *really* gross us out are the ones that combine the worst of all worlds.

In other words, diseases that **a)** *really* alter your life functions, **b)** have *visible* signs or symptoms, and **c)** can be *easily caught* from others.

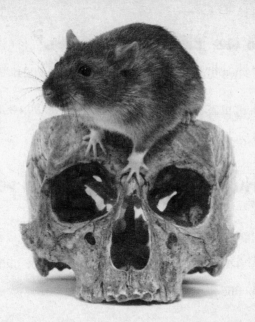

For this reason, we are far more grossed out by **infectious** (catchable) diseases like **rabies**, **leprosy** and **bubonic plague** than **non-infectious** diseases such as **cancer**, **diabetes** and **heart disease**. In the developed world, at least, the latter three are far more

In 1665, an outbreak of bubonic plague spread by rat fleas killed 15 per cent of London's population. There are still thousands of cases of plague every year worldwide.

common (and deadly). But because we can't *catch* them from other people, they lose their 'yuck' factor immediately.

In fact, leprosy and plague aren't even *that* infectious. But they *look* very nasty, and they *can* be caught. So for most of us, they're *gross enough* . . .

How do we 'catch' diseases?

Ever heard the phrase 'Watch out — there's a bug going round!'?

What a silly phrase. As if there was just one bug making everybody sick.

But I thought bugs DID make people sick.

It's true that 'bugs' (bacteria and viruses) can and do cause disease. And sometimes a single strain of virus can make a lot of people in one area sick.

The **influenza** virus, for example, seems to appear and reappear every winter, striking down thousands with '**a dose of the flu**' that lasts anywhere from three days to three weeks.

If your 'flu' lasts for less than that, then it probably wasn't the flu. It was probably just a nasty cold.

Outbreaks happen when a particular virus or bacterium infects lots of people in a short time, causing an explosion in the number of sick people in a certain area. A disease outbreak in a single village, city or country is

called an **epidemic**. An outbreak that goes worldwide is called a **pandemic**.

Epidemics happen all the time, but **pandemics** are (thankfully) rare. The last great flu pandemic happened in 2009, when the H1N1 'swine flu' virus spread across Asia and into Europe, Australia, Africa and the Americas. It infected millions and killed around 280,000 people worldwide.

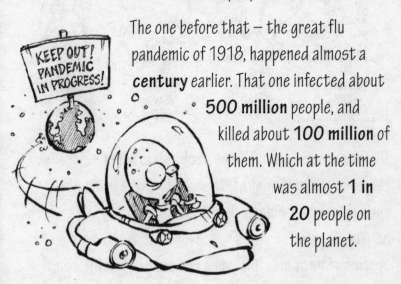

The one before that – the great flu pandemic of 1918, happened almost a **century** earlier. That one infected about **500 million** people, and killed about **100 million** of them. Which at the time was almost **1 in 20** people on the planet.

So if these 'killer bugs' are always going around, then why haven't they killed us all off already? And where do they go in the years between outbreaks and pandemics?

The simple truth is, these 'bugs' have *always* been around. Bacteria, or something like them, were the first forms of life to evolve on Earth – at least **3.5 billion years** ago. That's about **3.2 billion years** before the dinosaurs, and about **3.4 billion years** before the first mammals (which only showed up about **160 million** years ago).

3.5
BILLION
YEARS
AGO

240
MILLION
YEARS
AGO

65
MILLION
YEARS
AGO

200,000
THOUSAND
YEARS
AGO

The oldest were probably the **archaebacteria** — strange single-celled bugs that still survive today in boiling-hot springs, volcanic magma vents and super-salty lakes where *nothing* else can survive. These evolved into thousands of species of **bacteria**, including rod-shaped **bacilli**, spiral **spirochetes**, blob-like **cocci** and many, many more.

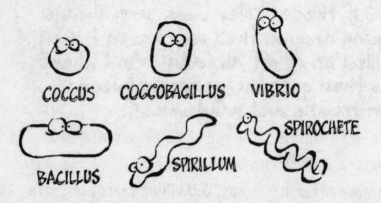

COCCUS   COCCOBACILLUS   VIBRIO

BACILLUS   SPIRILLUM   SPIROCHETE

It was the **bacteria** that transformed our atmosphere — sucking in **methane** and **carbon dioxide**, spitting out the **oxygen** and paving the way for the plants, animals and fungi that followed.

Wow - so bacteria are like our great-great-great-great-grandparents?

In a way. And they still live with us — in the **soil**, in the **ocean**, in the **lakes** and **rivers** we drink from and **inside the bodies** of every living thing on the planet.

Some bacteria are **helpful** to us. They live in our guts and on the surface of our skin, helping us to digest food and crowding out harmful bugs that would otherwise infect us. We call these bacterial 'good' guys **symbionts**.

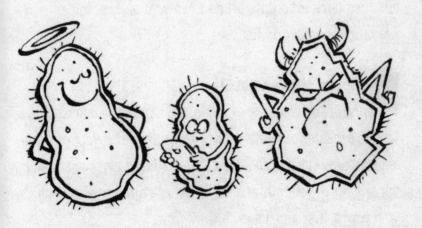

Others **neither help us, nor harm us**. They live in (or on) our bodies, feeding off our body wastes, minding their own business, and rarely (if ever) making us sick. We call these tiny, harmless loafers **commensals**.

The rest are **parasites** that **live it up at our expense**. As they feed and grow inside and upon our bodies, they steal our nutrients, damage our immune systems or otherwise weaken our essential life functions. These bad boys are the bringers of **disease**.

Good guys, bad guys and harmless loafers. If it was that simple, it would be a lot easier to avoid bacterial diseases. But unfortunately many bugs can occupy more than one of these roles. While some (called **obligate parasites**) are full-time bad guys, others start as **symbionts** or **commensals**, but then **turn into parasites** when your body becomes weakened by injury or disease.

What do you mean?

Eschericia coli bugs, for example, are harmless commensals that live inside your guts in their **billions**. But if your gut wall is punctured (by a stab wound, or speeding bullet), then they spread out of your gut and infect other organs — damaging your heart, liver and lungs as they grow.

Likewise, *billions* of harmless **Staphylococcus aureus** (SA) bugs live on the surface of your skin day in, day out, with ever doing any harm. But if you have an operation in a grubby hospital (or one that overuses antibiotics), they may turn into MRSA 'superbugs' that enter your wounds and do massive, even deadly damage inside the body.

Yep – even if you shower twice a day. They grow back within hours.

Most bugs, then, are *chancers*, or *opportunists*. They'll live with you when it suits them. But they'll eat you if they can . . .

What about viruses? How do they do damage?

All viruses are parasites. They cannot copy themselves without hijacking the machinery inside living cells. So their only goal is to evade your immune system and copy themselves as quickly and as often as possible. Most are very good at it too. But depending on the type of virus – and which cells they choose to infect – the effects of having a virus might vary from a **snotty nose** to **deadly fevers** and **death**.

Rhinoviruses and **adenoviruses** infect the cells of your ears, nose, throat and lungs, causing common colds that last anywhere from 24 hours to several weeks. **Hantaviruses** infect the same cells but spread to your blood cells and organs, making them burst apart as they break free. As you can see, there's quite a difference.

The point is, bacteria and viruses have been around a *lot* longer than we have, and they will most likely *still be here* long after we're gone. Or at least, as long as there are still living things left to infect.

They're not *trying* to make us sick. There isn't just one bug 'going round' each season, in an otherwise bug-free world. The agents of disease are all around us, all the time.

So while it makes sense that we're disgusted by nasty diseases and their symptoms, there's nothing particularly revolting about the things that cause them.

The bugs are just doing what they do. It just so happens that sometimes that's not so much fun for us . . .

True or False: Dreadful Diseases

Infection by bacterial and viral parasites can be a *nasty* business. Cast your eyes over this little list of horrors, and see if you can work out which diseases are **real** and which ones are simply **made up**.

Botulism

A fatal disease caused by food bacteria, which first **paralyses your eyelids**, **eyebrows** and **mouth**, and later your **lungs**, causing **respiratory failure** and **death**.

Hydrophobia

A deadly disease caused by a virus found in wild dogs, bats and foxes. When passed to humans, it infects the brain, causing **paralysis**, **fear of water** and **death** within a week.

Scabies

A contagious skin infection carried by tiny **mites**, which **burrow and multiply beneath the skin**, causing **itchy scabs** to appear all over the body.

Smallpox

A highly contagious disease marked by small, **fluid-filled blisters** that erupt all over the body. Later these may burst and bleed, causing **fevers**, **blindness** and **death**.

Largepox

An infectious disease similar to smallpox, but which causes **blisters the size of footballs**, and is far more deadly.

Walking Corpse Syndrome

A strange disease in which the sufferer **believes himself** (or herself) to be **dead**, or an undead **zombie**.

Unicorn Syndrome

A contagious disease carried by **head lice**, which results in the growth of **long, horn-like structures** from the centre of the forehead.

Spiderman Syndrome

A virus carried by certain spiders which, when passed to humans, causes the growth of **thousands of sticky hairs** on the **palms** and **soles of the feet**, allowing the sufferer to stick to walls and trees.

Tree Skin

A viral disease which causes **woody, bark-like growths** to form all over the hands, forearms and other parts of the body, making you look like a **human tree**.

Stone Man Syndrome

Horrific disease in which your **skin**, **muscles** and **tendons** gradually **turn into bone** – slowly crippling and trapping you inside your own body like a **human statue**.

Smurf Disease

An odd disease that **turns your skin** entirely and permanently **blue**, like a Smurf.

Werewolf Disease

Rare disease that results in the growth of **thick mats of hair all over the body**, making the sufferer look like a **werewolf**.

Beetlemania

Brain disease transmitted by the bites of bark beetles, which infects the **brain** and makes the sufferer feel like he or she is *covered with beetles*.

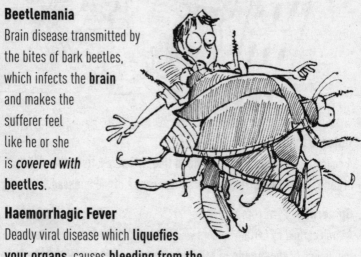

Haemorrhagic Fever

Deadly viral disease which **liquefies your organs**, causes **bleeding from the nose**, **eyes** and **skin** and **kills over 90 per cent** of those who catch it.

Flesh-Eating Bacteria

A horrific skin disease in which **bacteria** infect the skin and begin **eating through your flesh**, leaving **massive, gaping holes** in your arm, leg, or wherever the infection formed. The only treatment is to **cut the flesh away** faster than the bug can eat it.

Answers on page 154

Maggots, Worms and Parasites

Would You Rather...

- Be bitten by bedbugs or tasted by ticks?
- Have a fish inside your nose or a maggot beneath your skin?
- Have a huge worm living in your bottom or a tiny worm living in your eye?

Although most infectious diseases are caused by **bacteria** and **viruses**, there are *plenty* of other disease-causing parasites in the world.

Disease causing para-whats?

As we've already learned, **parasites** are creatures that **live inside or upon other living things**, feeding and multiplying themselves at the host's expense.

Gross!

Parasites are *everywhere* in Nature, and come in all shapes and sizes. There are parasitic **plants**, parasitic **fungi**, parasitic **insects**... even parasitic **birds**.

Of which the cuckoo is the most famous. Cuckoos lay their eggs in the nests of other birds. So baby cuckoos are — technically — sly birdy parasites feeding off parents that are not their own.

Parasites exist in every kingdom of life, and in every one — from bacteria to animals — **parasites outnumber non-parasites by at least four to one**.

In other words, **four out of every five organisms** on the planet is living off something else. Some even argue that even **humans** are parasites, living off the giant organism we call Earth. Have a think about that one later . . .

Setting aside bacteria and viruses, there are three main classes of parasite that commonly cause sickness in humans. These are **protozoa**, **helminths** and **arthropods**.

Attack of the Micro-Bugs!

Protozoa are microscopic creatures that belong to the kingdom **Protista**. Being super-tiny and single-celled, **protozoa** look a lot like bacteria. But they have different cell structures, and **move themselves around** inside their hosts (as opposed to bacteria, which simply drift and plop on to things, and grow wherever they settle).

*Zoologists divide all living things on the planet into six 'kingdoms' of life. These are **Archaea** (ancient bacteria), **Bacteria**, **Protista**, **Fungi**, **Plantae** (plants) and **Animalia** (animals).*

Parasitic protozoa come in a range of shapes and families, which include:

- **amoebas**, which squidge around using blob-like feet called **pseduopodia**
- **flagellates**, which propel themselves through blood and water using thread-like propellers called **flagella**, and
- **ciliates** – which swim by rippling the little hairs (called **cilia**) that cover their body.

Many protozoa are harmless to humans. But the nasty ones (like *Giardia* and *Plasmodia*) cause diarrhoeal diseases, or blood disease such as **malaria**. The *really* nasty ones (like *Naegleria*) actually eat your brain!

Attack of the Flatworms!

Helminths are **parasitic worms** that range in size from microscopic to several metres long! There are three major groups of helminths:

Nematodes are microscopic **worms** that live inside the body of pretty much every plant and animal on the planet (including you). There are so many, in fact, that if you made the bodies of every plant and animal **completely invisible**, you would *still* be able to make out their shapes and outlines, due to the *billions* of nematodes that fill their tissues.

Parasitic nematodes include **Ascarids** (roundworms), **filiaria** (threadworms), **hookworms** and **pinworms**. These can all cause disease in animals by blocking the guts, hearts, arteries and blood vessels. When the vet gives a '**de-worming**' pill to your pet cat or dog, these little wormy parasites are the target. Thankfully, though, nematodes from cats and dogs don't survive well in humans, so we rarely get diseases from our pets.

Cestodes are ribbon-like **tapeworms** with long, flat bodies. Some cestodes are tiny, others are enormous. They occupy the guts of living animals and steal food by absorbing nutrients through their skin. Again, many cestodes are harmless — about half the population of the world has one of these worms and doesn't even know it. Some worms might even *help* us digest things and fight off infections. But others cause disease by stealing our nutrients, producing toxins or simply clogging up our digestive systems with their sheer numbers.

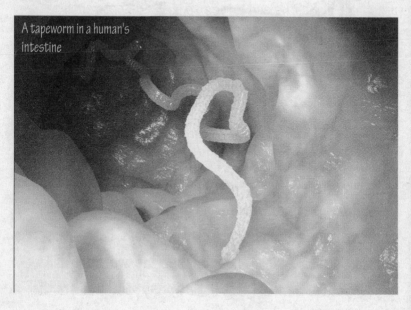

A tapeworm in a human's intestine

Trematodes are leaf-shaped **flukes** which glide through the bloodstream of a host and attach themselves to organs and blood vessels using sticky suckers. They cause a range of lung, liver, blood and gut diseases in humans, including the deadly **sleeping sickness** (**schistosomiasis**) that infects over 200 million people every year in Africa.

Attack of the Vampires!

Parasitic **arthropods** are small animals with outer shells (exoskeletons) and jointed legs, which range in size from tiny arachnids like **ticks** and **mites** to larger insects such as **wasps** and **flies**.

Though this class of animals also includes larger things, such as **tarantulas**, **lobsters** and **giant Japanese spider-crabs**, these larger arthropods cannot live upon us or inside us, so don't bother humans as parasites.

Instead, we get bitten by **mosquitoes**, **sandflies**, and **tsetse flies**, which feed off our blood like tiny vampires. Worse yet, our beds and clothes become infested with ticks, mites and bedbugs, which feed off blood and dead skin.

And a few species even lay their eggs inside us, which hatch into fat maggots that wriggle and crawl around beneath our skin.

Ugh!

Many arthropods also carry smaller disease-causing creatures (such as nematodes and flatworms) inside them, bringing even more parasites to the party!

Ecto versus Endo

The first two classes of parasite – **protozoa** and **helminths** – are known as **endoparasites**, because they live **inside** our bodies (*endo* means 'inside' in Latin). The third, **arthropods**, usually bite or live on the **outside** of our bodies, so they're known as **ectoparasites** (you guessed it, *ecto* means 'outside').

Perhaps because we can *see* them living on us, the **ecto** – (**outer**) **parasites** seem far more horrific than their hidden, **endoparasite** cousins.

Don't believe me? Then cast your eyes over *this* little list of lovelies.

If your skin isn't crawling by the end of it, then you may be destined to be a parasitologist!

Top 10 Horrifying Parasites

1 **Bedbugs** *(Cimicidae)* – Blood-drinking parasitic insects that live in cosy bird nests, bat caves and human bedrooms. Human bedbugs travel around by clinging to clothes, carpet fibres and the fur of pet animals. They feed mostly at night, causing itchy, red splotches wherever their bites break the skin. Washing (even steam-cleaning) does little to remove a bedbug infestation once it is established. In fact, they can cause hotels to shut down for weeks, while the bugs are gassed out. One old wives' remedy for bedbugs – scattering bean leaves on the floor – has recently been proven to work. The leaves trap the feet of the bedbugs like flypaper.

2 **Tapeworm** *(Cestoda)* –Long, flat worms that infect human guts, and remain there, stealing your food for weeks, months, or even years. Tapeworm eggs are eaten with undercooked meat or water contaminated by faeces, and hatch into larvae that hook on to the gut wall. There they grow, letting your food wash over them, and absorbing nutrients through their porous bodies. There are thousands of tapeworm species found worldwide. The most common ones in the Western world are the pork tapeworm (*Taenia solium*), beef tapeworm (*Taenia saginata*) and dwarf tapeworm (*Hemynolepis nana*). Tapeworms are mostly harmless, but can cause tiredness, weight loss, gut pain and diarrhoea. They are treated with anti-helminthic drugs, which remove the worm within a day or two.

*Pork and **beef** tapeworms come, as you might expect, from undercooked pork and beef. **Dwarf** tapeworms come from all kinds of contaminated food (as opposed to undercooked dwarfs).*

3 **Guinea Worm** *(Dracunculus)* – The largest parasite known to infect human beings, the guinea-worm larva lives inside tiny water fleas that slip into humans in contaminated water. Inside your stomach, the water flea melts away, leaving only the tough, round worm behind. The adult worm grows to **1 metre** or more (some are longer than your leg), and burrows out of your gut. Eventually it reaches the surface of your skin, where it creates a burning blister. When you seek relief, by dunking your blisters in cool water, the worm escapes and lays fresh eggs. These are eaten by water fleas and the hideous cycle continues . . .

4 **Giant Roundworm** *(Ascaris lumbricoides)* – A massive **nematode** worm that infects the human intestine. You get them by drinking water contaminated by human faeces. The worm's eggs pass from faeces to water, then into the gut of the drinker. There they hatch into larvae and quickly grow into adult worms. An infected intestine may contain hundreds of adult *Ascaris* worms.

From there, they may burrow through the intestine into the bloodstream and travel to the liver, heart and lungs, where they are coughed up or pooped out into water, and the cycle repeats. Giant roundworms infect up to 1.2 *billion* people globally, mostly in tropical regions. Which means up to one-sixth of the entire human population of the planet has one!

5 **Threadworms** *(Filaria)* – *Filaria* is the name given to a range of thread-like **Nematode** worms (*filum* means 'thread' in Latin) that live mostly in Africa, Asia and the Pacific islands. Different threadworm species cause different types of disease. Some simply cause sores and blisters on the skin, while others lead to **river blindness**. The nastiest, perhaps, causes **lymphatic filariasis**. This worm enters your body through a mosquito bite, growing, multiplying and clogging up your **lymph nodes**. This causes a painful and hideous-looking condition called **elephantiasis**. Doctors can prevent this disease using drugs that kill the worm larvae. But once you have adult worms (and full-on elephantiasis) there is no known cure.

Not 'elephantitis', as many people believe it is called.

6 **Eye Worm** *(Loa loa)* – Another type of filarial worm, common in Central and Western Africa, which infects humans through the bite of the deer fly. Once inside the body, the tiny worm matures into an adult and may crawl around beneath your skin for years before it is detected. Then one day you feel something strange and itchy, look in the mirror and see it **wriggling away inside your eye**. These horrid eye worms are not particularly dangerous – mostly they just cause painful swelling beneath the skin wherever they crawl. But unless killed with medicines or removed by surgery, they can survive inside your skin (or eye) for **up to 17 years**.

7 **Vampire Fish** *(Candiru)* –A horrifying name for a truly horrifying animal. Also known as the **toothpick worm**, this tiny parasitic catfish lives in the jungle rivers of the Amazon. It mostly feeds on the blood of other fish. But it has been known to dart into the nose (or bottom, or any other opening) of unlucky humans wading into in its habitat. There, it spreads its sharp, spiny gills, wedging itself inside and feasting on your blood. It can only be removed by a rather painful operation. Ouch!

8 **Human Botfly** *(Dermatobia hominis)* –Hideous
insect that lays its eggs on female mosquitoes. The
eggs then fall into open mosquito bites and hatch
into **bots**, (aka **maggots**). These maggots **live
under your skin for 5–12 weeks**, then burrow
their way out, drop to the ground and turn into adult
botflies. To remove the maggots, you must tape over
the entry wound to cut off its air supply. This
makes them poke their heads out, so you can
grab them with tweezers and pull them –
slowly and painfully – from your skin. Whatever you do, *never* type in
'Botfly Removal' on YouTube. You have been warned.

9 **Leishmania** –Single-celled parasites of the family *Trypansoma*,
which are passed to humans via sandfly bites and burrow into skin
and internal organs. The ones that stay in the skin cause **cutaneous
leishmaniasis**, a tropical disease than affects over 2 million people
each year. This is rarely deadly, but causes massive, unsightly skin
lesions, often confused with **leprosy**. Leishmania parasites have been
known to eat right through the facial tissue of sufferers, leaving them
without an ear or nose.

10 **Brain-Eating Amoeba** *(Naegleria)* –Single-celled protists
that swim in warm ponds, lakes and rivers. There they wash
into the noses of unfortunate human swimmers and use their arm-like
pseudopodia to swim, crawl and burrow into your head, where they feed
on your bacteria, your blood cells and (if you're unlucky enough) your
brain tissue. The result? Headaches, loss of your sense of smell, fevers,
vomiting and (if left untreated) death within two weeks. Truly this bug is
the stuff of nightmares . . .

Icky Science Expert 4

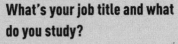

I study zombie roadkill worms.

Dr James Flowers,
North Carolina State University

What's your job title and what do you study?

I'm a Professor of Helminth Ecology. In short, I study the growth and behaviour of parasitic flatworms which live inside the bodies of wild animals.

How does your job benefit the world?

Well, my lab research helps establish critical facts and info about parasites, so that other scientists can develop anti-parasitic drugs and treatments. I also lecture at the university, teaching students who want to become vets all about animal parasites. This makes them better able to treat pets, farm animals and wild animals infected with harmful parasites later on.

What first got you interested in science?

Being raised on a farm, I always enjoyed looking at animals, especially wildlife. I was fascinated by mammals, birds, reptiles, amphibians, bugs, critters and dinosaurs – though sadly we didn't have any dinosaurs on the farm.

I had the adventurous curiosity of a nineteenth-century naturalist – I loved the idea of collecting, describing and naming 'new' species.

While studying zoology at NC State University, I took a work-study job with a parasitologist named Dr Grover Miller, who introduced me to the world of worms.

I realized that the helminths (flatworms) that infect humans, cats and dogs had been thoroughly studied. But hardly anyone had looked at the worms that affect common North American wildlife, like raccoons and opossums. At least, not in any detail! I had found my own little unexplored world – the world of wildlife worms!

These worms came in a huge range of shapes and sizes. Their life cycles and behaviours were all different too. This made my new world very exciting. I would literally find a new species in almost every roadkill body I looked at.

That's the part some people would find gross, I suppose. Here in the US, hundreds of raccoons and opossums venture on to busy roads by night and are run down by speeding vehicles. I collect this fresh 'roadkill' and study the bodies for worms. (That way, I don't have to harm any live animals in order to study their parasites.)

Typically, each body contains three to seven different worm species, with at least one *new* form found in every opossum!

It might not be as glamorous as discovering an unknown bird or monkey. But it's still kind of cool to think that you're discovering a new or little-known species, every day.

What's the most disgusting thing you've ever seen or done in connection with your job?

For one parasitology class, I collected some roadkill opossums and froze them. After about two months in the freezer, we thawed the carcasses, then necropsied them – cut them open – to see the worms frozen inside. But get this – some of the Physaloptera (stomach worms) we found immediately came back to life, and started wiggling their way out of the body. Attack of the zombie worms!

PHEW! THAT WAS CLOSE!

CONCLUSION
Eek! Get Away from Me!

So what have we learned on this journey into all things disgusting?

We've learned that **disgust** is linked to **digestion** and our fear of eating foods that might harm us. This is why retch at the thought of rotten meat, curdled milk and maggoty cheese.

We've learned that **disgust** is linked to **danger** and our fear of unfamiliar, poisonous and venomous animals. This is what keeps us away from befriending slugs, salamanders, venomous snakes and spiders. Well, *most* of us anyway . . .

We've learned that **disgust** is linked to **disease** and our fear of infection with harmful bacteria, viruses and parasites. This is why we're fine with our *own* bodily fluids (containing our own bugs), but can't stand the thought of *other people's* snot, drool and sweat all over us. Or worse yet, their bug-laden blood, pus or poo . . .

Finally, we've discovered that **disgust** can be both **learned** and **unlearned**. And this may be the most important discovery of all.

After all, **not all weird foods are harmful**. Some — like *natto*, *kimchi* and organ meats — might actually be very good for us.

Likewise, **not all snakes, spiders and salamanders are dangerous**. In fact, very few of them are. And some of them need friends right now. Worldwide, one in three amphibian species is at risk of extinction. Snakes aren't faring much better. So if we can't get over our misplaced fear and disgust, we might be too late to protect them.

Perhaps most importantly of all, **not all diseases are contagious**. So while disgust helps us keep diseases at arm's length, it makes us fear and shun the **victims** of disease, too. Often with very hurtful effects. Doctors and nurses can't afford to be disgusted by illness. The same goes for the rest of us, when our friends and loved ones get sick.

In short — **you shouldn't always trust your disgust**. It can be fun to gross yourself out, thinking about edible spiders, explosive diarrhoea and maggots that burrow under your skin. But we shouldn't get carried away with it. Making fun of real people with diseases, and treating them as if *they* are disgusting, is never a clever thing to do.

The good news is, we humans are pretty smart creatures, and we get to *decide* what to do with our disgust. We can give into it, and run from anything that grosses us out. Or we can conquer it, and become doctors, dentists, vets and scientists. We can be snake experts, frog experts and experts of tropical diseases. Looked at another way, disgust can lead to fascination, and fascination to a whole world of exciting science and medicine.

So ask yourself now — which way will *you* go?

Gross Out - the Card Game!

Did you enjoy grossing yourself and your friends out with this book?
Did you have fun pondering the **Would You Rather . . .?** questions at the beginning of each chapter?
Then visit **www.glennmurphybooks.co.uk** to find out how you can play **Gross Out** – an icky, yucky card game that goes perfectly with this book!

Answers

Page 80: Know Your Poop

```
              C       F
          M A N U R E
              S       A
          S C A T I N
          P   A   I   G
          R       N   S
    C     A       G
D R O P P I N G S
  U   W       N
  N   P       T
  G U A N O
      A
      T
```

Page 134: True or False

Botulism (TRUE)

Botulism is a rare (but deadly) disease caused by the bacterium *Clostridium botulinum*. You can get it from eating contaminated food (often canned meat or fish), whereupon the bacterium enters your bloodstream and produces deadly **Botulinum toxins** that paralyse nerves and muscles. Incredibly, these same toxins are injected (in smaller doses) into the faces of vain wealthy people to remove wrinkles, during **Botox** treatment!

Hydrophobia (TRUE)

Hydrophobia (which means 'fear of water') is another name for rabies. The disease gets its name from its symptoms, which include drooling, paralysis of throat muscles and a terror of drinking water (which causes painful spasms in the throat). The rabies virus is largely unknown in the UK, but still kills around 55,000 people each year worldwide – mostly in Asia and Africa.

Scabies (TRUE)

Scabies (not related to rabies) is caused by the *Sarcoptes scabiei* skin mite. In the worst cases, thousands of mites form thick crusts on the skin – occupying every part of the body except the face. Nasty.

Smallpox (TRUE)

Smallpox is caused by the *Variola* virus and has killed billions across the globe since ancient times. Thankfully, smallpox was wiped out worldwide by a global vaccination that took place from 1950 onwards. The last known case was in 1977, and the World Health Organization confirmed it was *gone* in 1980. Hooray! Let's hear it for science!

Largepox (FALSE)

Thankfully, smallpox has been wiped out, and there's no such thing as 'largepox'.

Walking Corpse Syndrome (TRUE)

Weird as it sounds, this is a rare but very real condition. Usually the result of an inborn brain defect (but sometimes, the result of brain damage), Walking Corpse Syndrome (also known as **Cotard's syndrome**) happens when the part of the brain that **recognizes faces** becomes disconnected from the brain's **emotional centres**. The result is that when you look in the mirror, you don't recognize your own face. Nor even that the thing you are looking at is *alive*. The logical explanation is that you are alive, but not alive (i.e. a zombie). Some sufferers also report feeling like they are rotting away, or cannot be killed. Weiiiiiird, eh?

Unicorn Syndrome (FALSE)

Unicorn syndrome does not exist. But there is a similar disease called **hyperkeratosis** or '**devil horns**'. That one is caused by the *Human Papilloma Virus* (HPV), which can cause hard hairy 'horns' to grow from the ears, nose or backs of the hands. Creepy.

Spiderman Syndrome (FALSE)

Sadly, this one only exists in comics and movies. Sigh.

Tree Skin (TRUE)

Incredibly, this one is real too. It results from a rare DNA mutation that makes you extra-vulnerable to the (otherwise harmless) Human Papilloma Virus (HPV). In most people, HPV simply causes small unsightly warts. But in a rare few, the warts take over the skin – turning your arms and legs into a **mass of bark-like growths**. The 'bark' fills the gaps between your fingers and toes, leaving you crippled and unable to walk or grab things. Nasty.

Stone Man Syndrome (TRUE)

This terrifying – but extremely rare – disease goes by the Latin name *Fibrodysplasia ossificans progressiva* (FOP). It is a genetic disease (i.e. one you're born with) – the result of a mutation that kicks your body's bone-sculpting mechanism into overdrive. Ordinarily, bone growth is kept in check by special proteins, keeping the formation of hard, chalky (**ossified**) bone tissue restricted to the bones, while softer, more flexible **cartilage**, **tendons** and **connective tissue** form *around* them. But in sufferers of FOP, these soft tissues start to ossify too, slowly hardening into bone over the course of a decade or so. In the end, you literally turn to stone, with only the lips left moving.

Worse yet, trying to **cut away** the bone tissue only results in *more* bone being formed, as the body tries to 'repair' itself after surgery – speeding up the **'stonification'** process. Yikes.

Smurf Disease (TRUE)

Otherwise known as *argyria*, 'Smurf disease' is caused by drinking silver solutions, or inhaling silver dust. The disease is very rare among regular folks. But it is most common among **miners** and fans of 'natural' medicine.

Werewolf Disease (TRUE)

Yep. This one's real too. The technical name for it is *generalized hypertrichosis*. It's the result of a genetic disorder that makes thick, dark **terminal hairs** grow all over your skin, rather than just the areas (armpits, groin, chest, back and chin) where they usually appear.

Beetlemania (FALSE)

Nope. This one doesn't exist either. Although there is a similar condition called **Morgellon's disease**, in which sufferers believe their skin to be covered with (or invaded by) crawling bugs. That one isn't an infectious disease passed on by beetles, though. It's inborn.

Haemorrhagic Fever (TRUE)

A range of nasty **hantaviruses** – Including the famous **Ebola virus** – cause this horrifying disease, which really does liquefy your organs and make you bleed to death through your skin. The only 'good' thing about these viruses is that they kill their victims so rapidly that they have no time to spread beyond the remote African villages where these diseases are most common. If one of these viruses ever made it to a big city, we'd be in *trouble*.

Flesh-Eating Bacteria (TRUE)

Though a range of 'flesh-eating' bacteria do exist, the most common is **Methycillin-Resistant Staphylococcus Aureus** (**MRSA**) – a harmless skin bacterium which sometimes becomes resistant (even **invulnerable**) to antibiotics. When such a bacterium infects a wound, it causes **Flesh-Eating Disease** (**necrotizing fasciitis**), as the skin, muscles and connective tissues (**fascia**) are eaten away by the rampaging superbug. Left untreated, this can be lethal.

Picture Credits

All photographs Shutterstock except for the following: page 6 Wikimedia Commons/Shardan, page 98 Wikimedia Commons/James Gathany and page 106 Wikimedia Commons/Bruce Wetzel and Harry Schaefer. All photographs of Icky Science Experts supplied and reproduced courtesy of the scientist in question.